ENVIRONMENTAL LAW

by
Margaret C. Jasper, Esq.

Oceana's Legal Almanac Series:
Law for the Layperson

1997
Oceana Publications, Inc.
Dobbs Ferry, N.Y.

You may order this or any other Oceana publications by visiting Oceana's website at http:\\www.oceanalaw.com

344.73046
J39e
2   V.16

ISBN: 0-379-11246-9 (alk. paper: acid-free paper)

Manufactured in the United States of America on acid-free paper.

22.50   AGR-4954

To My Husband Chris

**Your love and support
are my motivation and inspiration**

—and—

In memory of my son, Jimmy

ABOUT THE AUTHOR

MARGARET C. JASPER is an attorney engaged in the general practice of law in South Salem, New York, concentrating in the areas of personal injury and entertainment law. Ms. Jasper holds a Juris Doctor degree from Pace University School of Law, White Plains, New York, is a member of the New York and Connecticut bars, and is certified to practice before the United States District Courts for the Southern and Eastern Districts of New York, and the United States Supreme Court.

Ms. Jasper has been appointed to the panel of arbitrators of the American Arbitration Association and the law guardian panel for the Family Court of the State of New York, and is a New York State licensed real estate broker and member of the Westchester County Board of Realtors, operating as Jasper Real Estate, in South Salem, New York.

Ms. Jasper is the author and general editor of the following legal almanacs: Juvenile Justice and Children's Law; Marriage and Divorce; Estate Planning; The Law of Contracts; The Law of Dispute Resolution; Law for the Small Business Owner; The Law of Personal Injury; Real Estate Law for the Homeowner and Broker; Everyday Legal Forms; Dictionary of Selected Legal Terms; The Law of Medical Malpractice; The Law of Product Liability; The Law of No-Fault Insurance; The Law of Immigration; The Law of Libel and Slander; The Law of Buying and Selling; Elder Law; The Right to Die; AIDS Law; Obscenity, Pornography and the Law; The Law of Child Custody; The Law of Debt Collection; Consumer Rights Law; Bankruptcy Law for the Individual Debtor; Probate Law; Victim's Rights Law; Animal Rights Law; Workers' Compensation Law and Employee Rights Law.

TABLE OF CONTENTS

INTRODUCTION

The health of our environment—the world in which we live—depends upon how we treat it. Our personal health very much depends upon the health of our environment. In other words, we need each other. The cleanliness and safety of the air we breathe and the water we drink are directly related to how well we safeguard our world.

Unfortunately, many either do not care or realize how important our actions are, and how present mistreatment and neglect of our environment—by both individuals and businesses—will come back to haunt us in the future, for generations to come. We have already witnessed the pollution of our waterways and our air. Rivers which were once great sources of fishing and recreational activities have become polluted, acidic pools of useless water. Decades of discharging chemicals into the atmosphere has made it nearly dangerous to breathe in many areas of the country.

For this reason, federal, state and local agencies have had to enact legislation to protect our natural resources from pollution and degradation, and to remedy the problems which already exist. This almanac defines the role of the United States Environmental Protection Agency and its subdivisions in achieving these objectives.

In addition, this almanac presents an overview of environmental law, including a general discussion of important environmental issues, including air pollution, water pollution, hazardous materials and wastes, wetlands preservation, and endangered species. Further, efforts to bring industry into compliance with the environmental mandates, including incentives available for self-auditing, are also discussed.

The Appendix provides the text of applicable statutes, directories of relevant agencies, a table of acronyms and abbreviations commonly used in environmental law, and other pertinent information and data. The Glossary contains definitions of many of the terms used throughout the almanac.

CHAPTER 1:

AN OVERVIEW OF ENVIRONMENTAL LAW

In General

In the past decade, significant legal issues concerning our environment have emerged. The practice of environmental law is rapidly expanding. Lawyers are frequently hired to represent parties in a wide array of environmental matters, e.g. to assist clients in complying with the statutory mandates; to bring legal action against—or to defend—violators.

Individuals are concerned that the air they breathe and the water they drink is kept clean and safe. Developers are concerned about land use legalities, such as building in wetland areas. The federal, state and local governments have enacted legislation to address these concerns and protect our environment.

Historical Background

Although most significant environmental legislation has been enacted in the past several decades, historically, there have always been common law remedies for a variety of environmental concerns. For example, the common law doctrine of *riparian rights* refers to the privileges enjoyed by landowners relating to waterways which flow through their property. Under the common law doctrine of *public nuisance* it is illegal to cause or permit a condition to exist which injures or endangers the public health, safety or welfare. Similarly, under the common law doctrine of *private nuisance*, it is illegal to destroy or deteriorate an individual's property, or interfere with an individual's lawful use or enjoyment of their property.

In large part due to public awareness about the uncertain future of our environment, Congress began to enact statutes dealing with specific environmental issues, such as air pollution, water pollution, hazardous waste, etc. This almanac focuses on the primary federal environmental statutes.

Federal Jurisdiction

In enacting legislation governing certain environmental issues, Congress preempted jurisdiction over these areas. Nevertheless, Congress further provided that state and local governments could enact similar environmental protection legislation provided the standards were equal to—or surpassed—the federal legislation, and could continue their control over such issues provided they operate within the Federal framework.

For example, many local governments have enacted their own statutes concerning environmental issues, such as land use and historic preservation. Therefore, it is important for the reader to check the law of his or her own state and local jurisdiction in addition to the federal statutes.

A table of acronyms and abbreviations commonly used in Environmental Law is set forth in the Appendix.

CHAPTER 2:

THE ENVIRONMENTAL PROTECTION AGENCY

In General

The United States Environmental Protection Agency (EPA) is the federal agency responsible for protecting public health. This is accomplished in large part by improving the natural environment upon which human life depends, e.g the air, land and water. The EPA ensures that the federal environmental laws are implemented and enforced.

A directory of regional EPA offices is set forth in the Appendix.

As further discussed below, the EPA is comprised of a number of subdivisions which handle specific environmental issues and problems.

The Office of Enforcement and Compliance Assurance

The Office of Enforcement and Compliance Assurance (OECA) is responsible for making sure those subject to regulation are in compliance with the law. In order to do so, the OECA provides compliance assistance and incentives, and uses regulatory enforcement tactics.

Regulatory Enforcement

In enforcing the law, the EPA has collected the largest penalties ever from those who pollute the air, the water, and the land in violation of the law. Its regulatory enforcement programs are administered by The Office of Regulatory Enforcement (ORE); the Office of Criminal Enforcement, Forensics, and Training (OCEFT); and the Federal Facilities Enforcement Office (FFEO). These offices are responsible for developing enforcement policies, and bringing civil or criminal enforcement actions.

The Air Enforcement Division

The Air Enforcement Division (AED) is that part of the OECA/ORE responsible for judicial and administrative enforcement activities under the Clean Air Act (CAA), including the 1990 Amendments to the Act; and the Noise Control Act (NCA). The AED's Mobile Source Program enforces national motor vehicle fuel and emissions standards. The Stationary Source Program oversees woodstoves, acid rain, and stratospheric ozone protection.

The AED provides technical, scientific and engineering support; participates in and manages case negotiations; prepares litigation and settlement documents; and presents federal cases in administrative and court proceedings, including administrative or judicial appeals. The AED is the primary authority on all enforcement aspects of programs related to the Clean Air Act, and is primarily responsible for enforcement-related rulemaking. In addition, AED is responsible for reviewing Citizen Suits and amicus briefs submitted pursuant to the Clean Air Act.

The topic of air pollution is further discussed in Chapter 3 of this almanac.

The Water Enforcement Division

The U.S. Environmental Protection Agency's Water Enforcement Division (WED) operates within the OECA/ORE. The WED is responsible for The Clean Water Act (CWA), the Safe Drinking Water Act (SDWA), the Marine Protection, Research, and Sanctuaries Act (MPRSA), and the Oil Pollution Act (OPA). In that connection, the WED is involved with and enforces programs which address the following water pollution concerns: (i) The NPDES Program; (ii) Pretreatment; (iii) Sludge; (iv) Wetlands/Dredged and Fill Material; (v) Oil Pollution/Spills; (vi) Public Water System Supervision; and (vii) Underground Injection Control.

The WED also reviews citizen enforcement actions; participates in regulatory development and interpretation; and develops national enforcement policies, including settlement policies and policies encouraging pollution prevention, environmental justice, and innovative enforcement programs.

The WED works closely with other OECA offices, the EPA's Office of Water (OW), the EPA's Office of General Counsel (OGC), its Regional Offices, the States, and the Department of Justice on water enforcement matters.

The topic of water pollution is further discussed in Chapter 4 of this almanac.

Hazardous Wastes and the Resource Conservation and Recovery Act Enforcement Division

Pursuant to the Resource Conservation and Recovery Act (RCRA), the role of the Resource Conservation and Recovery Act Enforcement Division is to oversee the national hazardous waste enforcement program. They are responsible for protecting citizens from unacceptably high health risks caused by hazardous wastes. In that connection, they also serve as a national clearinghouse for legal and technical advice, information, and data, so as to bring industry into compliance. The division takes enforcement action against violators, and oversees administrative and judicial appellate litigation.

The topic of hazardous and solid wastes is further discussed in Chapter 5 of this almanac.

The Toxics and Pesticides Enforcement Division

The Toxics and Pesticides Enforcement Division (TPED) operates within the OECA/ORE. Its employees handle case development, policy and enforcement issues pursuant to the Federal Insecticide, Fungicide, and Rodenticide Act (FIFRA), the Toxic Substances Control Act (TSCA), and the Emergency Planning and Community Right-to-Know Act (EPCRA).

The responsibilities of TPED include: (i) coordination of national enforcement case initiatives; (ii) development of nationally significant cases; (iii) development of toxics and pesticides policy/guidance documents affecting case development and litigation; (iv) participation in regulatory workgroups; (v) promotion of supplemental environmental projects; (vi) providing support to the regions and the states on regional and state cases; (vii) maintaining liaison with the criminal office; (viii) undertaking legislative work; (ix) pursuing case development training; and (x) coordination of these activities with the states, OECA, the Department of Justice, and other concerned federal agencies.

The Multimedia Enforcement Division

The Multimedia Enforcement Division (MED) operates within the OECA/ORE. Through the MED, the OECA coordinates existing multimedia enforcement programs nationwide, and promotes these programs at the state and regional level. The MED provides legal and technical support for enforcement activities, coordination for national cases, contractual support for case development, and serves as an information clearinghouse for multimedia enforcement issues.

The MED coordinates enforcement efforts against companies who have violations at multiple facilities, revises EPA guidance documents, and improves coordination of penalty policies across different media programs. Multimedia enforcement is integral to the EPA's mandate to protect human health and the nation's environment.

The Federal Facilities Enforcement Office

The Federal Facilities Enforcement Office (FFEO) is that part of the OECA responsible for making sure that Federal facilities take actions necessary to prevent, control, and abate environmental pollution. The FFEO is composed of two groups: the Site Remediation and Enforcement Staff; and the Planning, Prevention and Compliance Staff. These two groups help to develop national policy and guidance related to compliance and enforcement issues confronting Federal facilities.

Criminal Enforcement

The Criminal Investigations Division (CID) is that part of the OECA responsible for criminal enforcement of federal environmental statutes. The CID investigates the most serious and willful polluters who pose the greatest threat to human health and the environment. The CID also provides training to its employees and partners in international, federal, tribal, state, and local law enforcement.

There are approximately 178 special agents employed by the CID nationwide. According to the CID's 1995 statistics, it initiated 548 cases; referred 262 cases to the Department of Justice and various states; handled 221 defendants; and obtained penalties—including jail time totaling 93 years —and 76.7 million dollars in criminal fines.

The CID participates nationwide in a multitude of environmental crime task forces. Its partners in these task forces consist of other federal law enforcement agencies, the U.S. Attorney's office, as well as state and local law enforcement and environmental agencies.

Small Business Compliance Assistance Centers

The EPA has made an effort to assist small businesses in complying with the environmental standards. National Small Business Compliance Assistance Centers were established for four specific industries which are comprised of a large number of small businesses. These four industries—printing, metal finishing, automotive services and agriculture—face substantial federal regulation. The Small Business Compliance Assistance Centers provide small business owners in these industries with detailed, comprehensive and easily understandable information on compliance with federal environmental laws. In addition, penalties have been lowered for small business owners who commit to correcting environmental problems.

⌣Environmental Violation Complaints

Individuals who have tips or complaints concerning an environmental matter are advised to contact their Local or State Environmental Agency, or one of the EPA's Departmental Hotlines. A Directory of EPA departmental hotlines is set forth in the Appendix.

CHAPTER 3:

AIR POLLUTION

In General

All Americans are concerned that the air they breathe is clean and healthy. Air pollution can make your eyes, nose and throat burn. More significantly, some chemicals that have been released into the air have been linked to cancer, brain damage, nerve damage, birth defects and serious respiratory illness. In fact, some air pollutants may even cause death.

Air pollution also adversely affects the environment. It has damaged and destroyed foliage and harmed animals. Air pollution has damaged the ozone layer which protects the Earth from harmful rays. This in turn can cause illnesses, such as skin cancer and cataracts. Air pollution also destroys property. For example, it erodes stone, dirties property, and can cause a dangerous visibility-reducing haze.

Improving and protecting the quality of our air is a national goal which requires the cooperation and efforts of many agencies, organizations and industries, as well as the public.

The primary source of legislation relating to air quality is found in the Clean Air Act, as further discussed below.

The Clean Air Act (42 U.S.C. 7401 et seq.)

In General

In an effort to improve air quality, Congress enacted The Clean Air Act in 1970. Major changes to the original Act were made with the passage of The 1990 Clean Air Act Amendments—the most recent version of the law. The 1990 Clean Air Act is a comprehensive statute which attempts to address all aspects of the complex problem of air pollution. It contains seven separate titles covering different regulatory programs. The term Clean Air Act as used in this almanac refers to the 1990 Clean Air Act.

As further discussed below, the Clean Air Act covers some of the most pressing environmental problems facing Americans today, such as acid rain, toxic air emissions and urban air pollution. In addition, the Act established a national permit program, and strengthened enforcement capabilities.

State Involvement

Although the 1990 Clean Air Act is a federal law, the states carry much responsibility in administering the Act. The law recognizes that solving pollution problems in various areas often requires a special understanding of the local area, including its geography and industry. To assist the states in developing successful clean air programs, the EPA provides funding and services, e.g., scientific research and engineering services.

The Act sets a maximum threshold on how much of a pollutant can be in the air. This standard applies to the entire country to ensure that all individuals have the same basic health and environmental protections. Nevertheless, the individual states are permitted to have their own air pollution laws, provided their standards are equal to or more stringent than the federal law.

It is an established fact that air pollution can travel across state borders. Thus, the Clean Air Act includes provisions designed to reduce interstate air pollution, and provides for interstate commissions on air pollution control. These commissions are responsible for developing regional strategies for cleaning up air pollution.

Of course, air pollution can also move across national borders. The Clean Air Act addresses that problem as well, and includes provisions designed to reduce pollution that originates in Mexico and Canada and drifts into the United States, as well as pollution from the United States that extends to Canada and Mexico.

Title I: Air Pollution Prevention and Control

Title I of the Clean Air Act is concerned with air pollution prevention and control. The task of keeping our air clean, and cleaning air that has become dirty, is the responsibility of the U.S. EPA's Office of Air Quality Planning & Standards (OAQPS). The OAQPS carries out their responsibilities by collecting data, undertaking research and analysis, and enforcing air quality standards. The Clean Air Act provides the regulatory framework within which the OAQPS operates.

The EPA has established six "criteria pollutants" as indicators of air quality. These pollutants are commonly found all over the country, and are known to cause harm to health, and damage to the environment and property. Common criteria air pollutants include smog, carbon dioxide, and particulates—e.g., soots, dusts, and smoke.

The OAQPS has further established a maximum concentration of these criteria pollutants. The OAQPS monitors air quality standards by measuring concentrations of criteria pollutants. These measurements are taken at nationwide monitoring stations. Any levels above the established maximum concentration are deemed to have adverse effects on human health.

One set of limits—known as the primary standard—protects health. Any levels above the established maximum concentration limits are deemed to have adverse effects on human health. Another set of limits—known as the secondary standard—addresses environmental and property damage.

These maximum limits are known as National Ambient Air Quality Standards (NAAQS). A geographic area that meets or does better than the National Ambient Air Quality Standard is called an attainment area. If an area does not meet this standard, it is called a nonattainment area. It has been estimated that about 90 million Americans live in nonattainment areas.

Under the Act, each state is required to develop a written plan for cleaning the air in their areas. This plan, called a State Implementation Plan (SIP), sets forth the steps the state is going to take to improve air quality and to keep clean air from deteriorating. The states must involve the public, through hearings and opportunities to comment, in the development of each state implementation plan.

The SIP must be approved by the EPA. If a state fails to develop an acceptable plan, the EPA is entitled to take jurisdiction over enforcement of the Clean Air Act for that state.

On an annual basis, the EPA examines the air pollution trends of the six criteria pollutants and releases a document setting forth a detailed analysis of changes in air pollution levels over the last 10 years time, plus a summary of the current air pollution status. This document is known as the National Air Quality and Emissions Trends Report.

A chart of common air pollutants is set forth in the Appendix.

Title II: National Emissions Standards - Mobile Sources of Pollution

Title II of the Clean Air Act is concerned with the emissions standards for mobile sources of air pollution. A mobile source is one which is able to move, e.g. cars, trucks, and buses. These vehicles emit large amounts of hazardous pollutants into the air, and are the primary source of the urban smog problem.

Smog consists of ground-level ozone. Although ozone located high above the earth protects us, ground-level ozone is harmful. Ground-level ozone is produced by the combination of hazardous pollutants, including exhaust fumes.

Smog forms as the pollutants are blown through the air by the wind. Because the wind blows the smog-forming pollutants away from their sources, smog may be more severe far away from the source.

Smog forms more easily when it is hot and sunny. The pollutants literally "cook" in the air. The severity of smog depends very much on the weather and geographical factors. For example, when warm air stays near the ground instead of rising—known as a temperature inversion—and winds are calm, smog may remain for days.

Efforts to produce cleaner fuels and engines, and to make sure that pollution control devices operate efficiently, are expected to reduce hazardous air pollutants from mobile sources. In fact, cars today produce up to 80 percent less pollution than in the 1960's.

For the most part, leaded gasoline has been discontinued, causing a significant decline in air levels of the toxic chemical. Nevertheless, motor vehicles are still responsible for up to half of the smog-forming VOCs and nitrogen oxides (NOx), releasing more than 50 percent of the hazardous air pollutants, and up to 90 percent of the carbon monoxide found in urban air.

To address this problem, the Clean Air Act has endeavored to reduce the pollution caused by motor vehicles. The law calls for using cleaner cars and fuels and requiring auto inspections to make sure automobiles are maintained.

In order to make a significant dent in automobile pollution, cleaner fuels must be developed. Under the Clean Air Act, gasoline refiners must reformulate the gasoline sold in the smoggiest areas so it contains less volatile organic compounds (VOCs), such as benzene—a hazardous air pollutant that causes cancer and aplastic anemia.

To combat carbon monoxide pollution in certain areas, refiners will have to sell oxyfuel—gasoline with oxygen added to make the fuel burn more efficiently—thereby reducing carbon monoxide release. Further, all gasolines will have to contain detergents to keep engines working smoothly and burning fuel cleanly. The Clean Air Act also encourages the development of alternative fuels such as alcohols, liquefied petroleum gas, and natural gas.

The Clean Air Act requires car manufacturers to build a certain number of cars which use cleaner fuels, and electric cars, which are low in pollution. By 1999, at least 500,000 of these clean fuel cars are to be manufactured for sale yearly in California—the state with the worst smog problem.

The law also requires cars to have under-the-hood systems and dashboard warning lights that check whether pollution control devices are working properly. The law extends the working life of these pollution control devices from 50,000 miles to 100,000 miles.

Smaller trucks are subject to similar requirements as automobiles. Large diesel trucks and buses are required to be manufactured in such a way as to reduce particulate releases by at least 90 percent.

In addition to cleaner fuels and cars, the law also requires that vehicles undergo periodic inspection and maintenance to makes sure the pollution emissions are kept at a low level.

Title III: Toxic Air Pollutants

Title III of the Clean Air Act is concerned with toxic air pollutants. According to the EPA, more than 2.7 billion pounds of toxic air pollutants are emitted annually in the United States, and such exposure has been linked to 1000 to 3000 cancer deaths each year. Toxic air pollutants have also been linked with the destruction of the protective ozone layer.

To remedy this problem, the Act sets forth a list of 189 hazardous air pollutants selected by Congress on the basis of potential health and/or environmental hazard. The EPA is required to regulate these listed air toxics. The EPA is also permitted to add new chemicals to the list as it deems necessary.

To regulate hazardous air pollutants, the EPA must identify categories of sources that release the 189 chemicals listed by Congress, such as gas stations, chemical plants, etc. The air toxics producers are further classified as either large or small sources.

Once the categories of sources are listed, the EPA issues regulations, in some cases setting forth exact specifications on how to reduce air pollutant releases. The pollution sources are required to use the Maximum Available Control Technology (MACT)—a very high level of control—to reduce releases.

Sources which want to increase the amount of air toxics released may choose to "offset" the increases so that their total hazardous air pollutant releases do not exceed their limitations. They may also choose to install pollution controls to keep pollutants at the required level.

An example of a commonly used source of toxic air pollutants is the woodburning stove. Woodburning stoves have become popular sources of inexpensive heat. Unfortunately, the smoke produced from the stove often contains particulates, such as soot and dust. The stoves also emit higher levels of hazardous air pollutants than smoke from oil or gas furnaces, and some of these pollutants have been linked to cancer. There has been an effort to redesign woodburning stoves so that they emit less pollution into the air. In that connection, the Clean Air Act has authorized the EPA to issue guidelines for the reduction of pollution from woodburning stoves.

Title IV: Acid Air Pollutants

Title IV of the Clean Air Act is concerned with acid air pollutants—commonly known as "acid rain." Acid air pollutants are harmful to our health and property, and damaging to the environment. The Clean Air Act has devised a program to reduce acid air pollutants.

The main source of acid rain are pollutants emitted from coalburning power plants. The coal contains sulfur which becomes sulfur dioxide (SO2)when the coal is burned. The larger the power plant, the more sulfur dioxide released into the air. These power plants also release nitrogen oxides (NOx). SO2 and NOx are chemicals related to sulfuric acid and nitric acid, two very strong acids.

These harmful pollutants are released into the air and carried by winds. If the wind blows the acid chemicals into areas of the country which experience wet weather, the acids actually become part of the precipitation, e.g., rain, snow or fog. If the wind blows the acid chemicals to dry areas of the country, they fall to the earth in dust or gas form.

When the acidic precipitation falls into waterways, such as lakes and streams, the water becomes very acidic. This in turn harms and destroys plant and animal life. Acid rain also makes the air hazy or foggy. Acid rain does more than environmental damage; it can damage health. Acid air pollution has been linked to severe respiratory problems.

To combat this problem, the Clean Air Act requires that by the year 2000, annual releases of sulfur dioxide will be reduced at least 40 percent, which should cause a major decrease in acid rain. The total sulfur dioxide releases for power plants will be permanently limited to the level set by the Clean Air Act for the year 2000.

In achieving this goal, the Clean Air Act has taken a market-based approach. Power plants may only release as much sulfur dioxide as they have "allowances" to do so. If a plant expects to release more sulfur dioxide than it has allowances, it has to obtain more allowances. They can buy or trade for more allowances from other power plants which have reduced their sulfur dioxide releases.

Every power plant is required to utilize continuous emissions monitoring systems which monitor the amount of SO2 and NOx being discharged. There are severe penalties for plants which release more pollutants than their allowances permit. Conversely, the law awards bonus allowances to power plants who assist in the effort to reduce sulfur dioxide, e.g. by using renewable energy, such as solar energy, or by installing cleaner coal technology.

Title V: Permit Program

Title V of the Clean Air Act established an operating permit program for larger sources of air pollution, e.g. power plants and factories. This permit program is modeled after the Federal National Pollution Elimination Discharge System (NPDES). The purpose of the permit program is to ensure compliance with the Clean Air Act, and to strengthen the EPA's enforcement capabilities. Businesses seeking permits have to pay permit fees which are used to pay for state air pollution control activities.

Requiring polluters to apply for a permit is not unique. Approximately 35 states have already implemented permit programs for air pollution. Under the EPA program, the permits are issued by the states. However, if a state fails to carry out the Clean Air Act provisions, the EPA can take over the permit issuance process.

The permit must include information on all types of pollutants being released; the quantity of each pollutant; and the source's pollution monitoring and reduction plan. Thus, the program ensures that all of a source's responsibilities relating to its pollutants will be contained in one permit document. This program assists the Federal and state agencies in its evaluation of the air quality situation.

As further discussed in Chapter 5, The Clean Water Act also requires permits for the release of pollutants into lakes, rivers or other waterways.

Title VI: Stratospheric Ozone and Global Climate Protection

Title VI of the Clean Air Act is concerned with depletion of the ozone layer and global climate protection. Most people have heard about "holes" in the ozone layer. The ozone layer is a protective shield situated approximately 10 to 30 miles above the earth. It filters out harmful rays from the sun, such as the UV rays that have been linked with skin cancer. An ozone hole is not really a "hole" in this protective layer, but a thinning or worn area. Some ozone holes which have been discovered are as large as the mainland United States.

Several decades ago, aerosol cans were linked with destruction of the ozone layer due to their use of propellants known as chlorofluorocarbons (CFCs) which were released into the air. As a result, the use of CFCs as propellants in aerosol cans was banned.

The Clean Air Act is concerned with repairing these ozone holes, however, this is a long-range task. A number of countries have already agreed to reduce production of chemicals that harm the ozone layer. However, there is no quick solution to repairing the ozone layer. The Clean Air Act sets forth a schedule for ceasing the production of ozone damaging chemicals.

Because a large number of consumer products contain ozone destroying chemicals and other harmful chemicals, they are subject to regulation under the Clean Air Act. Those products with the most damaging chemical make-up are required to label their product with a warning that the product "contains or is manufactured with [the name of the chemical], a substance which harms public health and the environment by destroying ozone in the upper atmosphere." Products with a lesser damaging chemical make-up will have to be in compliance with the warning label by the year 2015.

Title VII: Enforcement

Title VII of the Clean Air Act is concerned with enforcement of its provisions. The Act contains a variety of authorities which make it more readily enforceable, as is the case with the other major environmental statutes.

The Act has empowered the EPA by strengthening their enforcement capabilities. The EPA has been given new authorities to issue administrative penalty orders of up to $200,000, and field citations up to $5000 for lesser infractions. The Act provides for greater civil judicial penalties, and the criminal penalties for willful violations have been upgraded from misdemeanors to felonies.

In addition, the Act allows private citizens the right to bring a citizen suit for penalties against a source, or the government, if the law is not enforced. The penalties go to a U.S. Treasury fund for use by EPA for compliance and enforcement activities.

CHAPTER 4:

WATER POLLUTION

In General

Prior to 1972, America's water resources were rapidly declining. The majority of the nation's waters were unsafe for recreational activities, such as fishing and swimming. Soil was being eroded as a result of agricultural runoff, resulting in massive deposits of phosphorus and nitrogen into the waters. People were rightfully concerned about the safety of their drinking water. In response to public concern over the safety and cleanliness of our nation's water, Congress enacted The Clean Water Act in 1972.

The Clean Water Act (33 U.S.C. 1251 et seq.)

In General

The Clean Water Act is the primary federal law protecting the integrity of our water. It is a comprehensive piece of legislation that has resulted in dramatic improvement in the quality of our water. The Act is carried out through the cooperative efforts of federal, state, local and tribal governments.

The goals of the Clean Water Act are to (i) eliminate the discharge of pollutants into our waterways, and; (ii) achieve and maintain water quality levels that are suitable for recreational activities, such as fishing and swimming.

The Clean Water Act carries out its objectives by: (i) maintaining strict standards on water quality, e.g. it requires industry to meet certain performance standards to ensure water pollution control; (ii) offering financial aid to assist in compliance with the law—e.g., it authorizes funding to state and local governments to help them meet their clean water infrastructure needs; and (iii) protecting valuable wetlands and other aquatic habitats—e.g., it operates a permit process to ensure that land development is conducted in a manner that is beneficial to the environment.

The EPA works closely with other interested federal, state and local parties in an effort to maintain the integrity of the nation's water, including state ground water, drinking water, and Clean Water Act personnel; representatives of water systems; watershed managers; environmental and public health advocates; and agricultural interests groups. These parties are given the opportunity to participate directly in development of EPA guidance and policy.

In addition, the EPA has established partnerships with other Federal agencies, drinking water utilities, and non-profit organizations, to assist in the implementation of EPA standards. For example, in 1995, the Partnership for Safe Water was formed. The Partnership is a voluntary joint venture comprised of the EPA, states, and several national organizations representing drinking water systems.

The partnership developed a program to accelerate public health protection from the bacteria known as "cryptosporidium," as well as other microbial contaminants. This was accomplished by implementing a program to improve water filtration plant performance. Water utilities that complete phases of the program receive recognition from their peers and the EPA for these voluntary activities to pursue water quality goals beyond the regulations. Over 200 utilities that provide water to approximately 85 million persons are members of the Partnership.

Three major provisions of the Clean Water Act are discussed below, including (i) the role of the National Pollutant Discharge Elimination System (NPDES) in protecting the nation's water, e.g., through its Permit Program which governs the discharge of wastes; (ii) The Oil Pollution Act, which sets forth the Federal government's authority relating to oil spills; and (iii) The Safe Drinking Water Act, which regulates and protects the integrity of the nation's drinking water.

The National Pollutant Discharge Elimination System

The NPDES Permit Program

The NPDES Permit Program is the mechanism by which the Clean Water Act ensures that there are no unauthorized discharges of pollutants into the nation's waters. The Act requires wastewater dischargers to obtain a permit. The permit establishes pollution limits, and specifies monitoring and reporting requirements. There are more than 200,000 sources regulated by NPDES permits nationwide.

The NPDES permits regulate household and industrial wastes that are collected in sewers and treated at municipal wastewater treatment plants. These permits also regulate industrial sources, and concentrated animal feeding operations, that discharge into other wastewater collection systems, or that discharge wastewater directly into receiving waters.

The goal of the NPDES permit program is to protect public health and aquatic life, and to make sure every facility treats their wastewater. The EPA uses a variety of methods to make sure permit holders comply with the conditions of their permits, such as conducting on-site inspections. If a regulated facility fails to comply with the provisions of its permit, it may be subject to enforcement actions.

Types of Regulated Pollutants

Pollutants regulated under the Clean Water Act fall under the categories of conventional pollutants and toxic pollutants, as further set forth below.

Conventional Pollutants

Conventional pollutants are those contained in the wastewaters of homes, businesses and industries. Conventional pollutants are commonly found in human waste, laundry and bath water; and sink disposal deposits. They may include (i) fecal coliform—a bacteria found in human and animal digestive tracts that may indicate the potential presence of pathogenic organisms in water; and (ii) oil and grease—organic substances comprised of hydrocarbons, fats, oils, waxes, and/or high-molecular fatty acids, which may produce sludge solids that are difficult to process.

Toxic Pollutants

Toxic pollutants are categorized as either (i) organic—e.g., pesticides, solvents, polychlorinated biphenyls (PCBs), and dioxins; or (ii) metals—e.g., lead, silver, mercury, copper, chromium, zinc, nickel, and cadmium. Toxic pollutants are particularly harmful to plant and animal life.

Nonconventional Pollutants

Nonconventional pollutants are any substances that do not fall into the above two categories, but which require regulation, such as the nutrients nitrogen and phosphorus.

The NPDES Watershed Program

The EPA's Office of Water Management (OWM) has developed the NPDES Watershed Strategy to ensure that watersheds are effectively protected. Under the Watershed Strategy, six areas have been identified that must be addressed to improve water quality: (i) Coordination with the states water protection programs; (ii) Streamlining the NPDES Permit Program; (iii) Developing state-wide monitoring strategy and requirements; (iv) Revising and updating existing national accountability measures; (v) Encouraging public participation in developing watershed protection plans and identifying local environmental goals; and (vi) Taking enforcement action against violators.

The NPDES Wet Weather Strategies

As set forth below, the NPDES is responsible for implementing wet weather strategies, such as (i) storm water management, and (ii) combined and sanitary sewer overflow control.

Storm Water Management

Storm water discharge from a number of sources is not easily controlled. Thus, the Clean Water Act has established a two-phased approach to remedying storm water discharges. Phase I of the program requires permits for separate storm water systems serving large and medium sized communities—i.e., those with over 100,000 inhabitants—and for storm water discharges associated with industrial and construction activity involving at least five acres.

Phase II of the program addresses remaining storm water discharges, such as those occurring in urban areas with populations under 100,000, smaller construction sites, and retail, commercial, and residential sites.

Combined and Sanitary Sewer Overflows

In 1994, the EPA issued a policy for the control of combined sewer overflows. Communities with combined sewer overflow problems are required to take immediate and long-term action to remedy the problem. This includes making sure that the sewer systems are operating properly, and receiving regular maintenance. In addition, a public notification requirement was included to ensure that the public receives prompt notification of the health and environmental impact of such overflows.

The EPA is currently in the process of evaluating the extent of sanitary sewer systems nationwide in an effort to identify any related issues which may pose a threat of harm to human health, property, and water quality.

The Oil Pollution Act (33 U.S.C. 2701 et seq.)

In 1990, Congress passed the Oil Pollution Act (OPA) in an effort to expand the prevention, preparedness, and response capabilities of the federal government and industry to oil discharges.

Oil spills pose serious threats to fresh water and marine environments. Oil spills adversely effect wildlife and their habitats. For example, the sad images of birds and mammals coated with oil and unable to function are often broadcast on the news following an oil spill.

In addition, the oil itself is toxic and poses a serious threat of harm, depending on the type of habitat. Some organisms may be seriously injured or killed very soon after contact with the oil, while other organisms suffer long-range effects, such as slow poisoning caused by long-term exposure to trapped oil.

Under Section 311(a)(1) of the Clean Water Act, "oil" is defined as "oil in any kind or in any form including, but not limited to, petroleum, fuel oil, sludge, oil refuse, and oil mixed with wastes other than dredged soil." "Navigable waters" are broadly defined to include all waters that are used in interstate or foreign commerce, all interstate waters including wetlands, and all intrastate waters, such as lakes, rivers, streams, wetlands, sloughs, prairie potholes, wet meadows, playa lakes, or natural ponds.

The OPA amends Section 311 of the Clean Water Act, to (i) clarify federal response authority; (ii) increase penalties for oil spills; (iii) establish U.S. Coast Guard response organizations; (iv) require tank vessel and facility response plans; and (v) provide for contingency planning in designated areas.

The OPA also establishes a new liability and compensation system for oil spills into navigable waters; provides resources for the removal of discharged oil; and merges the funds established under several other laws in order to create a national spill trust fund.

The Safe Drinking Water Act

The Federal Safe Drinking Water Act (SDWA) was first enacted in 1974. In 1996, Congress passed amendments to the SDWA in order to strengthen the Act's public health protection by broadening its scope of action and level of public involvement. The SDWA amendments emphasize comprehensive public health protection through regulatory improvements, increased funding, prevention programs, and public participation.

The existing law was improved in two important ways: First, the amendments focus on setting risk-based priorities., i.e. a decision on which contaminants to regulate will be based on data concerning the adverse health effects of the contaminant, its occurrence in public water systems, and the projected risk reduction. Public health protection remains the primary concern on which drinking water standards are based. Second, states have been given more flexibility to implement the Act to meet their specific needs. In addition, available funding has been increased through higher state drinking water program grants, and a new Drinking Water State Revolving Fund (DWSRF), designated for water system infrastructure improvements.

Providing safe water is a comprehensive and coordinated effort among the EPA, state, local and tribal governments, water suppliers, and the public. The amendments recognize that everyone has an interest in making sure the nation's drinking water is safe.

An important aspect of the amendments was the creation of the National Drinking Water Advisory Council (NDWAC). The NDWAC is a Federal advisory group whose role is to support the EPA's drinking water program by providing advice and recommendations to the EPA on drinking water issues. The NDWAC represents the drinking water community, including the public.

The SWDA amendments also established a microbial and disinfection byproducts advisory committee to assist the EPA in evaluating new data and information concerning microbial contaminants. Microbial contaminants, such as Cryptosporidium and Giardia, and byproducts of disinfection, have been identified as the highest potential drinking water risk to human health. The SWDA amendments have made the reduction of this risk a priority, and require the EPA to set (i) new limits for disinfection byproducts in drinking water; (ii) removal requirements for Cryptosporidium; and (iii) tighter standards for the cloudiness in suppliers' incoming water that may indicate microbial contamination.

In order to participate in the combined effort to maintain the integrity of our drinking water, individuals should familiarize themselves with the source of their drinking water, be aware of common indicators of contamination, and contact the appropriate authorities when a drinking water problem arises.

More than half of the nation's drinking water comes from underground wells. The rest of the drinking water comes from surface water sources, such as rivers, lakes and reservoirs. Tap water that meets the EPA and state standards is considered safe to drink. Thus, it is important to check whether the water supplier meets all of the required standards. The applicable state drinking water agency should be able to assist the consumer with this information.

Under the SDWA, water systems that service in excess of 25 people are required to test their water regularly for a wide variety of contaminants, some of which are discussed below.

Fecal Coliforms

Fecal coliforms are associated with sewage or animal waste. The presence of fecal coliforms in drinking water is usually caused by a problem with water treatment, or with the pipes that distribute the water. This may indicate that the water may be contaminated with organisms that can cause disease.

Lead

Lead is rarely in drinking water when it leaves the water treatment plant. Its presence in water usually comes from plumbing, particularly in older buildings that still have lead pipes. Children and pregnant women are most susceptible to health risks from lead in drinking water.

To reduce the amount of lead in drinking water, the EPA advises consumers to flush the cold water faucet by allowing the water to become cold before using it. One should never consume water from the hot water tap if lead is present. In addition, boiling only increases the concentration of lead in the water. You may be able to purchase a home water treatment unit that is designed to remove lead from the drinking water. Alternatively, use bottled water for drinking and cooking.

Copper

Blue-green water may be an indicator of high copper levels in the water. Adverse health effects of copper in the drinking water include stomach and intestinal distress, liver and kidney damage, and anemia. To reduce the amount of lead in drinking water, the EPA advises consumers to flush the cold water faucet by allowing the water to become cold before using it. One should never consume water from the hot water tap if copper is present. Hot water dissolves copper more quickly than cold water. You may be able to purchase a home water treatment unit that is designed to remove copper from the drinking water. Alternatively, use bottled water for drinking and cooking.

Radon

Radon is a soil gas that can affect underground sources of drinking water. The gas is known to cause lung cancer when inhaled at high levels over a long period of time. If you are concerned about radon in your drinking water, you may have your water tested by a state-certified lab. The EPA is currently working on proposing regulations for radon in drinking water. The proposed regulations are scheduled to be issued in August 1999.

Cryptosporidium

Cryptosporidium is a parasite commonly found in lakes and rivers. It enters water supplies through sewage and animal waste. It causes cryptosporidiosis, a gastrointestinal disease. The most common symptom of cryptosporidiosis is watery, non-bloody diarrhea, often accompanied by abdominal cramps, nausea, vomiting, fever, headache, and/or loss of appetite. Generally, the disease is mild and people recover within one to three weeks. However, the disease can be severe, chronic, and even fatal for people with seriously weakened immune systems.

If there is concern that drinking water is contaminated by radon, the EPA advises consumers to boil water before using it. You may be able to purchase a home water treatment unit that is designed to remove cryptosporidium from the drinking water. Alternatively, use bottled water for drinking and cooking.

If the water system discovers that the presence of contaminants exceeds the EPA safety standard, they are required to take immediate action to correct the deficiency, and to alert the public about the problem and what action should be taken.

Individuals interested in having their own drinking water tested can call their state drinking water agency for a list of certified water testing labs. Each state is required to keep a list of all state-certified labs. The EPA does not test water quality for individuals.

Relevant provisions of The Safe Drinking Water Act are set forth in the Appendix.

CHAPTER 5:

HAZARDOUS MATERIALS AND SOLID WASTES

In General

Years ago, the public was generally unaware of how dumping hazardous materials could affect their health and the health of the environment. The hazardous materials seeped into the ground, into rivers and lakes, and ultimately contaminated soil and groundwater. Many of these hazardous waste sites were subsequently abandoned, including landfills, warehouses, manufacturing facilities, and processing plants.

Finally, the public became aware of this serious health hazard. Their concern over the extent of the problem led Congress, in 1980, to enact The Comprehensive Environmental Response, Compensation and Liability Act (CERCLA) to eliminate the health and environmental threats posed by these hazardous waste sites. The U.S. Environmental Protection Agency (EPA) administers the Act through the Office of Solid Waste and Emergency Response (OSWER).

The Comprehensive Environmental Response, Compensation and Liability Act of 1980 (42 U.S.C. 9601 et seq.)

The Comprehensive Environmental Response, Compensation and Liability Act of 1980 (CERCLA)—commonly referred to as "The Superfund Program"—is the most aggressive hazardous waste cleanup program in the world. The purpose of the Superfund Program is to provide authorities the ability to respond to uncontrolled releases of hazardous substances from inactive hazardous waste sites that endanger public health and the environment. It involves constant vigilance concerning situations that affect public health and the environment.

The Superfund Program uses the best available science to determine risks at sites, and to develop more expedient and less expensive ways to clean up the sites. If possible, old hazardous waste sites are restored to productive use. The Superfund Program authorizes the EPA to identify and clean up abandoned or uncontrolled hazardous waste sites, and to recover costs from parties responsible for the contamination. The Program also established prohibitions and requirements concerning closed and abandoned hazardous waste sites, and established a trust fund to provide for cleanup when no responsible party could be identified.

CERCLA further provided for the revision and republishing of the National Contingency Plan (40 CFR Part 300). The National Contingency Plan sets forth the guidelines and procedures needed to respond to releases and threatened releases of hazardous substances, pollutants, or contaminants, and provides for the National Priorities List, a list of hazardous waste sites in the country that are eligible for extensive, long-term cleanup under the Superfund program.

To evaluate the dangers posed by hazardous waste sites, the EPA has developed a scoring system called the Hazard Ranking System. Sites that score high enough on the Hazard Ranking System are eligible for the National Priorities List.

In addition, a site may be proposed for the National Priorities List if the Agency for Toxic Substances and Disease Registry issues a health advisory for the site, or if a state chooses a site for its top priority list.

Hazardous waste sites have been discovered by local and state agencies, businesses, the EPA, the U.S. Coast Guard, and by concerned citizens. The public can report suspected or potential hazardous waste sites to the National Response Center Hotline or to their state and local authorities.

Emergency Response

Some situations involving hazardous waste are emergencies—such as those involving chemicals—and require immediate action. Emergency actions are designed to eliminate immediate risks to public health and safety.

Typical chemical emergencies may include train derailments, truck accidents, and incidents at chemical plants where there is a chemical release or threat of a release to the environment. Superfund's number one priority is to protect the people in communities near sites and their environment. The hazardous materials are removed from the site for treatment or proper disposal, or they are treated at the site to make them safe. The EPA then evaluates the site and determines whether additional cleanup is necessary.

Non-Emergency Situations

When a potential hazardous waste site is reported, the EPA investigates the site to determine what type of action is necessary. The EPA may interview local residents to find out more about the site's history, and whether it has caused any adverse effects on the population or the environment.

Some sites do not require any action, while others are referred to the state, or other agencies, for cleanup or further action. For sites which require EPA intervention, it tests the soil, water, and air to determine what hazardous substances were left at the site and how serious the risks may be to human health and the environment. The EPA uses the information collected to decide what type of action, if any, is required. Parties responsible for the contamination at the site are also permitted to conduct these assessments under close EPA supervision.

The EPA then prepares a Community Relations Plan based on discussions with local leaders and private citizens in the community, and sets up a local information file in the community so that the public can access information about the site. The file contains the official record of the site—known as the Administrative Record—as well as additional site-related information.

Early Action

Early action is taken when the EPA determines that a site may soon become a threat to the public or the environment. For example, there may be a site where leaking drums of hazardous substances could catch on fire.

Typical early action is taken to:

1. Prevent direct human contact with contaminants from the site;

2. Remove hazardous materials from the site;

3. Prevent contaminants from spreading off the site;

4. Provide water to residents whose drinking water has been contaminated by the site; or

5. Temporarily or permanently evacuate or relocate local residents.

Long-Term Cleanups

Early action can correct many hazardous waste problems and eliminate most threats to human health and the environment. Some sites, however, require long-term action. These sites were caused by years of pollution and may take several years, or even decades, to clean up.

Long-term cleanups are extensive and involve a number of steps. First, a detailed study of the site is done to identify the cause and extent of contamination at the site, the possible threats to public health and the environment, and ways to clean up the site. The EPA then develops what is called a Proposed Plan for Long-Term Cleanup, which is made available to the public, and to local and state officials for comment.

Once all concerns are addressed, the EPA publishes a Record of Decision, which describes their plan to clean up the site. The subsequent design and actual cleanup of the site is conducted by the EPA, the state, or by the parties responsible for the contamination.

The EPA regularly monitors every National Priorities List site to make sure it remains safe. If there is any indication that a problem has arisen, immediate action is taken to make the site safe again.

Superfund Participants

Superfund cleanups are very complex and require the efforts of many experts in science, engineering, public health, management, law, community relations, and numerous other fields. The goal of the process is to protect the public, and the environment, from the effects of hazardous substances. Community involvement is very important. The public has the opportunity and the right to be involved in—and to comment on—the cleanup work being undertaken.

The Technical Assistance Grant Program

The EPA values public input . It endeavors to assist concerned citizens in understanding the technical information relating to the cleanup of Superfund sites in their community, so that informed decisions can be made.

Under the Superfund law, the EPA can award communities grants, known as Technical Assistance Grants, of up to $50,000 per site. Technical Assistance Grants allow communities to hire an independent expert to help them interpret technical data, understand site hazards, and become more knowledgeable about the different technologies that are being used to clean up sites. More information about Technical Assistance Grants is available from a Regional EPA Community Involvement Coordinator.

Community Advisory Group Program

One of the ways communities can participate in site cleanup decisions is by forming a Community Advisory Group. A Community Advisory Group is made up of representatives of diverse community interests. Its purpose is to provide a public forum for community members to present and discuss their concerns related to the Superfund decision-making process.

Contact a Regional EPA Community Involvement Coordinator for more information about the Community Advisory Group Program.

Costs

Under the Superfund law, the EPA is able to make those companies and individuals responsible for contamination at a Superfund site perform, and pay for, the cleanup work at the site. The EPA negotiates with the responsible parties to get them to pay for the plans and the work that has to be done to clean up the site. If an agreement cannot be reached, the EPA issues orders to responsible parties to make them clean up the site under EPA supervision.

The EPA may also use Superfund Trust Fund money to pay for cleanup costs, and then attempt to get the money back through legal action. The Superfund Trust Fund was set up to pay for the cleanup of these sites. The money comes mainly from taxes on the chemical and petroleum industries. The Trust Fund is used primarily when those companies or people responsible for contamination at Superfund sites cannot be found, or cannot perform or pay for the cleanup work.

The Underground Storage Tanks Program

According to the EPA, more than 300,000 releases have been reported from Underground Storage Tank (UST) systems. These releases have been caused by leaks, spills and overfills from UST systems. Many have posed serious threats to human health and the environment. In particular, petroleum products contain many potentially hazardous and toxic chemicals. Fumes and vapors can travel beneath the ground and collect in areas such as basements, utility vaults, and parking garages where they can pose a serious threat of explosion, fire, and suffocation or other adverse health effects.

Gasoline leaks from service stations, are a common source of groundwater pollution. Because approximately one-half of the population of the United States relies on groundwater as their source of drinking water, groundwater pollution is a serious problem. Many municipal and private wells have had to be shut down as the result of contamination caused by releases from UST systems.

The mission of the UST program is to protect human health and environmental quality by requiring proper management of underground storage tank systems. Good tank management includes prevention, detection, and timely, cost-effective cleanup of releases. The two primary goals of the UST Program are prevention and cleanup, as set forth below:

Prevention

The EPA endeavors to prevent the creation of a new generation of leaking USTs. Reaching this goal requires that USTs be protected from corrosion, protected against spills and overfills, equipped to detect releases, and be properly installed and maintained. Under EPA regulations, USTs that do not already meet these requirements must be upgraded, replaced, or closed by December 1998.

Cleanup

The EPA endeavors to ensure that UST releases are detected and cleaned up promptly and cost-effectively to the extent necessary to protect human health and the environment. Regular monitoring of UST systems by owners and operators ensure that releases are promptly detected.

Definition of an Underground Storage Tank

According to the Code of Federal Regulations, an underground storage tank is defined as any one or a combination of tanks that have 10 percent or more of their volume below the surface of the ground in which they are installed. This definition includes the tank, connected underground piping, underground ancillary equipment, and containment system.

Federal UST Regulations

In 1984, Congress directed the EPA to develop regulations for underground storage tank systems. Not all UST systems are Federally regulated, although they may be regulated by the state or local agency that implements a UST program. The EPA's Office of Underground Storage Tanks (OUST) developed the Federal regulations which delegate UST regulatory authority to approved State programs. States with approved programs operate in lieu of the Federal regulations. There are currently 24 states with approved UST programs.

Federally regulated USTs meet one or more of the following criteria:

1. The UST has a capacity of more than 110 gallons;

2. The UST contains regulated substances defined as hazardous under the CERCLA, with certain exceptions;

3. The UST does not contain hazardous wastes regulated—i.e., listed or identified—under Subtitle C of the Solid Waste Disposal Act, or a

mixture of such hazardous waste and another regulated substance; and/or

4. The UST is not part of a wastewater treatment system that is part of a wastewater treatment facility regulated under section 402 or 307(b) of the Clean Water Act.

Under the Code of Federal Regulations (40 CFR part 280.11), the following groups of tanks are not included in the definition of a UST:

1. A farm or residential tank of 1,100 gallons or less capacity used for storing motor fuel for noncommercial purposes;

2. Tanks used for storing heating oil for consumptive use on the premises where stored;

3. Septic tanks;

4. Tank systems in pipeline facilities (including gathering lines) regulated under the Natural Gas Pipeline Safety Act of 1968 (49 U.S.C. App. 1671 et seq.), the Hazardous Liquid Pipeline Safety Act of 1979 (49 U.S.C. App. 2001, et seq.), or in an intrastate pipeline facility regulated under State laws comparable to the provisions of law referred to in the two previous clauses;

5. Surface impoundments, pits, ponds, or lagoons;

6. Storm water or wastewater collection systems;

7. Flow-through process tanks;

8. Liquid trap or associated gathering lines directly related to oil or gas production and gathering operations;

9. Tanks in underground areas such as basements, cellars, and mine-working drifts, shafts or tunnels, if they are located on or above the surface of the floor.

UST systems that are excluded from Federal UST regulation include the following:

1. USTs holding hazardous wastes listed or identified under Subtitle C of the Solid Waste Disposal Act, or a mixture of such hazardous waste and other regulated substances;

2. A wastewater treatment tank system that is part of a wastewater treatment facility regulated under 402 or 307b of the Clean Water Act;

3. Equipment or machinery that contains regulated substances for operational processes such as hydraulic lift tanks and electronic equipment tanks;

4. Systems with capacities of 110 gallons or less;

5. Systems that contain de minimus concentrations of regulated substances; and

6. Emergency spill or overfill containment UST systems that are expeditiously emptied after use.

Applicability of some of the Federal UST regulations has been deferred for the following systems, however, releases from these systems must still undergo corrective action:

1. Wastewater treatment tank systems;

2. Any UST systems containing radioactive materials that are regulated under the Atomic Energy Act of 1954 (42 U.S.C.2011 et seq.);

3. Any UST system that is part of an emergency generator system at nuclear power generation facilities regulated by the Nuclear Regulator Commission under 10 C.F.R. Part 50, Appendix A;

4. Airport hydrant fuel distribution systems; and

5. UST systems with field-constructed tanks.

USTs storing fuel solely for use by emergency power generators are deferred from only the release detection requirements.

Detecting UST Releases

Releases from UST systems can originate from one or more of the system components, as well as from spills and overfills. Because most of the components are buried underneath the ground, the owner/operator must rely on methods other than sight and smell to determine if a release has occurred, including recognition of the following warning signals:

1. Unusual operating conditions, such as erratic behavior of the dispensing pump.

2. Results from leak detection monitoring and testing that indicate a leak.

3. Reports from fuel delivery drivers; or

4. Complaints from neighbors about vapors in their basements or about water that tastes or smells like petroleum.

Any suspected release must be reported immediately to the state or local implementing agency. Quick action can minimize the extent of environmental damage, and the threat to human health and safety, and the responsible party's share of the cleanup cost.

The Hazardous and Solid Waste Amendments of 1984

The Hazardous and Solid Waste Amendments (HSWA) of 1984 broadened the scope of the RCRA, authorizing the EPA to regulate underground storage tanks (USTs) containing petroleum products and hazardous substances. The resulting UST program includes provisions governing corrective action, financial responsibility, release detection, and tank installation and closure.

Transitional Period

The EPA's program has now entered a transitional period in which the Federal role in supporting state and local programs will change and eventually diminish as the EPA's major objectives are reached. Nevertheless, the EPA expects to continue working with State and local agencies to implement and enforce UST requirements well beyond December 1998.

The Resource Conservation and Recovery Act (42 U.S.C. 6901 et seq.)

In 1976, to address the dangers hazardous wastes pose, Congress enacted the Resource Conservation and Recovery Act (RCRA). The Act established a national program to ensure that hazardous wastes are managed safely from the point of generation to final disposal ("cradle to grave"). The RCRA regulates the identification, transportation, treatment, storage, and disposal of solid and hazardous wastes. In implementing the Act, the EPA has created a complex regulatory framework addressing solid waste disposal and hazardous waste management.

The RCRA regulates such items as: (i) hazardous waste generators and transporters; (ii) land disposal restrictions; (iii) federal procurement of products that contain recycled materials; (iv) municipal solid waste landfill criteria; (v) solid and hazardous waste recycling; (vi) treatment, storage and disposal facilities; and (viii) waste minimization and hazardous waste combustion.

Although the RCRA mostly deals with hazardous waste, Congress also made provisions in the Act for state and regional solid waste management plans. As the space in landfills is used up, solid waste management has become an important environmental concern. Recycling and elimination of many of the sources of such waste needs to be undertaken in order to reduce the volume of solid waste production.

Some states have found ways to use solid wastes to their benefit. For example, incineration systems—known as resource recovery facilities—generate electricity by using heat from burning solid waste to produce steam. However, these facilities have raised other concerns, e.g. dioxin emissions.

The Office of Site Remediation Enforcement

The Office of Site Remediation Enforcement (OSRE) strives to protect human health and the quality of the environment by providing direction, evaluation, oversight and assistance for remediation enforcement at nonfederally owned sites subject to the RCRA, CERCLA, the Oil Pollution Act (OPA), and the UST Program. The OSRE provides the means for states to vigorously and effectively enforce these statutes. The OSRE's goal is to achieve prompt site cleanup and maximum liable party participation in performing and paying for cleanup in ways which promote environmental justice and fairness.

The Office of Solid Waste and Emergency Response

The Office of Solid Waste and Emergency Response (OSWER) provides agency-wide policy, guidance and direction for the EPA's solid waste and emergency response programs. The Office develops guidelines and standards for the land disposal of hazardous wastes and for underground storage tanks. The Office furnishes technical assistance in the development, management and operation of solid waste activities and analyzes the recovery of useful energy from solid waste.

The Office has also undertaken the development and implementation of a program to respond to abandoned and active hazardous waste sites and accidental releases, including some oil spills, as well as the encouragement of innovative technologies for contaminated soil and groundwater.

OSWER is comprised of the following offices:

    1. Chemical Emergency Preparedness & Prevention;

    2. Federal Facilities Restoration and Reuse;

    3. Hazardous Waste Technology Innovations;

    4. Oil Spill Program;

    5. Office of Solid Waste: Hazardous, Non-Hazardous & Special; and

    6. A Special Initiatives Office.

The Federal Insecticide, Fungicide and Rodenticide Act (7 U.S.C. 136 et seq.)

Under the Federal Insecticide, Fungicide and Rodenticide Act (FIRFA), the EPA is charged with regulating the manufacture and packaging of pesticides. The use of pesticides is strictly controlled, and public notice is generally required when pesticides have been applied in public areas, such as restaurants. Further, the EPA requires that all pesticides be registered, and labeled and packaged according to the requirements set forth in the Act.

The Emergency Planning and Community Right-to-Know Act (42 U.S.C. 11001 et. seq.)

In November of 1986, Congress enacted The Emergency Planning and Community Right-to-Know Act (EPCRA), in large part due to the extreme danger posed by the bulk storage of petroleum and hazardous substances, even in small quantities. In passing this law, Congress recognized the need for local and state officials to be aware of such potential hazards.

The EPCRA was also designed to help communities prepare for chemical emergencies that may result from leakages. It allows the public, and local and state governmental officials, access to information about potential chemical hazards, such as the location and volume of all storage sites. The EPCRA established emergency planning and reporting requirements for facilities that store hazardous chemicals.

Common EPCRA topics include: emergency planning; hazardous chemical inventory reporting; public access to chemical information; toxic chemical release reporting; and the toxic release inventory (TRI) database. Hotline EPCRA specialists also answer questions on the accidental release prevention provisions of the Clean Air Act.

CHAPTER 6:

WETLANDS

In General

Wetlands are generally defined as areas where the recurrent and extended presence of water at or near the soil surface is responsible for the kind of soils that form, and the plant and animal life that inhabit the area.

There is growing recognition of the important contributions wetlands make to our environment. Wetlands are so ecologically beneficial, that they have been compared to the tropical rain forests.

Importance of Wetlands

Wetlands improve water quality by filtering runoff and adjacent surface waters—removing or retaining its nutrients, processing organic wastes, and reducing sediment before it reaches open water—thus protecting our lakes, bays and rivers, as well as many of our drinking water sources. Wetlands function like natural sponges, storing water and slowly releasing it, helping to slow floodwaters and reduce erosion at the shorelines.

In addition, rare and beautiful species of plant and animal life have been found to inhabit wetland areas, as well as many commercially and recreationally valuable species of fish and wildlife. The U.S. Fish and Wildlife Service estimates that a large number of the threatened and endangered species rely directly or indirectly on wetlands for their survival. Wetlands are also a great source of natural products, including fish, timber, wild rice, and furs.

Identifying Wetlands

Generally, wetlands are lands where saturation with water is the dominant factor determining the nature of soil development in the area, and the types of plant and animal life inhabiting the area. Wetlands vary widely because of regional and local differences in such factors as climate, type of soil, topography, and vegetation, etc., and are found on every continent except Antarctica.

The term "wetlands" is the collective word used to refer to marshes, swamps, bogs, and similar areas found in flat vegetated areas; in depressions in the landscape; and between dry land and water along the edges of streams, rivers, lakes, and coastlines. Many "wetlands" only contain water for a short period of time. The rest of the time they appear to be dry land, making it difficult sometimes to identify a wetland area.

One method used to identify wetlands is to observe them in the growing season, when the upper part of the soil is saturated with water. It is at this time that soil organisms consume the oxygen in the soil and cause conditions unsuitable for most plants. These conditions cause the development of "hydric soils" which are different in color and texture. Plants that are able to grow in such conditions are called "hydrophytes." The appearance of hydric soils and hydrophytes indicates the presence of wetlands.

Common examples of wetlands include swamps, bogs and marshes. Less recognized examples include (i) vernal pools—pools that form in the spring rains but are dry at other times of the year; (ii) playas—areas at the bottom of undrained desert basins that are sometimes covered with water; and (iii) prairie potholes. A description of some of the important types of wetlands are set forth below.

Bogs

A bog is characterized by spongy peat deposits, a growth of evergreen trees and shrubs, and a floor covered by a thick carpet of sphagnum moss. The only water source for bogs is rainwater. Bogs have extremely low nutrient levels that form acidic peat deposits. Much of the acidity in bogs is due to sulfuric acid formed by the oxidation of organic sulfur compounds and from humic acids produced in the water. Bogs serve important ecological functions in preventing downstream flooding by absorbing direct precipitation and runoff, protecting water quality by intercepting and filtering runoff, and providing critical habitat for unique plant and animal life able to survive on the low-nutrient diet. Bogs are found in the northern hemisphere.

Bottomland Hardwoods

Bottomland hardwood forests are river swamps, found along rivers and streams generally in the broad floodplain of the southeast and south central United States. They are deciduous forested wetlands, made up of different species of gum and oak, which have the ability to survive in areas that are either seasonally flooded or covered with water much of the year. Bottomland Hardwoods serve a critical role in the watershed by reducing the risk and severity of flooding to downstream communities. In addition, these wetlands improve water quality by filtering and flushing nutrients, processing organic wastes, and reducing sediment before it reaches open water.

Fens

Fens are a type of open freshwater marsh. Fens receive nutrients from sources other than precipitation, e.g., upslope sources through drainage from surrounding mineral soils and groundwater movement. Unlike bogs, peats associated with fens are not acidic and have higher nutrient mineral levels, and are therefore able to support much more diverse plant and animal life. Like bogs, fens are found in the northern hemisphere. Fens also provide important benefits to a watershed, including preventing or reducing the risk of floods, improving water quality, and providing habitat for unique plant and animal life.

Prairie Potholes

Prairie potholes are depressional wetlands found primarily in the Upper Midwest. They are generally comprised of freshwater marshes. Some prairie pothole marshes are temporary, while others may be permanent. This region, because of the numerous shallow lakes and marshes, the rich soils, and the warm summers, is described as being one of the most important wetland regions in the world. The area is home to more than 50 percent of North American migratory waterfowl, with many species dependent on the potholes for breeding and feeding. Prairie potholes serve to reduce the risk and severity of downstream flooding by absorbing rain, snow melt, and floodwaters and slowly releasing it.

Vernal Pools

Vernal pools are naturally occurring depressional wetlands that are covered by shallow water for variable periods from winter to spring, but may be completely dry for most of the summer and fall. These wetlands range in size from small puddles to shallow lakes and are usually found in a gently sloping plain of grassland. Beneath vernal pools lies either bedrock or a hard clay layer that helps keep water in the pool. The unique environment of vernal pools provides habitat for numerous rare plants and animals that are able to survive the harsh conditions. Many of these plants and animals spend the dry season as seeds, eggs, or cysts, and then grow and reproduce when the ponds are flooded again. In addition, birds such as egrets, ducks, and hawks use vernal pools as a seasonal source of food and water.

Destruction of Wetlands

According to the EPA, over half of the nation's wetlands were lost between the late 1700s and the mid-1980s. About 100 million acres of wetlands remain today in the lower 48 States. From the mid-1970s to the mid-1980s, wetlands were lost at an annual rate of 290,000 acres per year.

It is a fact that losing or degrading wetlands can lead to serious consequences, such as increased flooding, extinction of species, and a decline in water quality. The growing concern about the importance of wetlands to our environment has led to a concerted effort by federal, state, local and tribal governmental officials to restore and preserve these natural areas.

The U.S. Environmental Protection Agency - Wetlands Division

The stated mission of the EPA's Wetlands Division is to encourage and enable others to act effectively in protecting and restoring the nation's wetlands and associated ecosystems, including shallow open waters and free-flowing streams.

In carrying out its mission, the Wetlands Division is primarily responsible for (i) establishing national standards; and (ii) assisting others to comply with those standards.

In order to most effectively restore and maintain the nation's wetlands, the EPA's Wetlands Division incorporates an integrated wetlands/watershed approach in much of its work with other interested agencies. A watershed—also called a drainage basin—is the area in which all water, sediments, and dissolved materials flow or drain from the land into a common river, lake, ocean, or other body of water. The wetlands are considered important elements of a watershed because they serve as the link between land and water resources.

An integrated watershed-based approach to water and wetlands protection considers the whole system, including other resource management programs that address land, air, and water, to successfully manage problems for a given aquatic resource. The integrated approach recognizes that the quality of the nation's wetlands and other water resources is directly linked to the quality of the environment surrounding these waters.

Wetland Regulation Under the Clean Water Act

For regulatory purposes under the Clean Water Act, the EPA and the U.S. Army Corps of Engineers have defined wetlands as "those areas that are inundated or saturated by surface or ground water at a frequency and duration sufficient to support, and that under normal circumstances do support, a prevalence of vegetation typically adapted for life in saturated soil conditions."

In protecting the wetlands, the EPA and the Corps of Engineers jointly (i) administer the Section 404 Permit Program pursuant to the Clean Water Act; and (ii) take enforcement action against violators.

The Section 404 Permit Program

Section 404 of the Clean Water Act establishes a program to regulate the discharge of dredged and fill material into waters of the United States, including wetlands. The program's objective is to prevent any discharge of dredged or fill material into wetlands or waters, if a practicable alternative exists that is less damaging to the aquatic environment, or if the discharge would cause a significant adverse effect on the nation's waters.

Regulated activities are controlled by a permit review process. An individual permit is usually required for potentially significant impacts. However, for most discharges that will have only minimal adverse effects, up-front general permits are often granted. Section 404(f) exempts some activities from regulation, including many ongoing farming, ranching, and silviculture practices.

The EPA and the Army Corps of Engineers jointly administer the Section 404 permit program. Other agencies, including the U.S. Fish and Wildlife Service, the National Marine Fisheries Service, and various state resource agencies have important advisory roles in the process.

If an individual permit is required, public notice must be issued by the Corps of Engineers within 15 days of receiving all permit information. The public notice describes the permit application, including the proposed activity, its location, and potential environmental impacts. The public notice also invites comments which must be submitted within a specified period of time. The application and comments are then reviewed by the Corps of Engineers and other interested Federal and State agencies, organizations, and individuals. The Corps determines whether an Environmental Impact Statement (EIS) is necessary. An EIS is a report which sets forth the proposed action; its impact on the environment and energy sources; available alternatives; and mitigation measures. The EIS is generally made available to the public for review and comment before a permit can be issued.

The Corps of Engineers evaluates the permit application based on the comments received, as well as its own evaluation. The permit decision is set forth in a document known as a Statement of Finding, which is also made available to the public.

Section 404 Enforcement

In addition to jointly implementing the Section 404 permit program, the EPA and the Corps of Engineers share Section 404 enforcement authority. Violations under Section 404 generally include (i) the failure to comply with the terms or conditions of a Section 404 permit; or (ii) the discharge of dredged or fill material into waters of the United States without a permit. Violators are subject to a wide variety of enforcement actions.

Administrative Enforcement

The EPA can issue administrative compliance orders requiring the violator to stop any ongoing illegal discharge activity and to remove the illegal discharge and restore the site. The EPA and the Corps can also assess administrative civil penalties of up to $125,000 per illegal action.

Judicial Enforcement

The EPA and the Corps of Engineers have the authority to take civil judicial action, seeking restoration and other types of injunctive relief, as well as impose civil penalties.

Criminal Enforcement

The EPA and the Corps of Engineers also have authority to bring criminal judicial enforcement actions for knowingly or negligently violating Section 404.

CHAPTER 7:

ENDANGERED SPECIES

In General

Species and habitat endangerment and extinction is one of the most urgent environmental problems facing society today. Habitat extinction is a critical part of the problem because species cannot live without their supporting environment. Thus, habitat extinction is causally connected to animal extinction. In fact, the leading cause of species endangerment and extinction is loss of habitat, which is primarily caused by mankind.

Another major cause of species endangerment and extinction involves the accidental or intentional introduction of a species into a new setting, thereby disrupting the delicate ecological balance of the existing habitat.

The third leading cause of species endangerment and extinction is overexploitation. Overexploitation refers to the use of a particular species at a rate that leads to endangerment or extinction of that species.

For example, according to the African Wildlife Foundation, the volume of world trade in ivory from 1980 to 1985 was 800 tons per year. In order to meet such a demand, approximately 90,000 elephants had to be killed yearly. This caused a depletion in the African elephant population. In 1979, there were approximately 1,300,000 African elephants in existence, whereas there are presently less than 650,000.

Although species extinction is historically a natural occurrence, it has increased at an unprecedented rate primarily due to human activity which does not allow for species adaptation. As a result, it is estimated that hundreds of thousands of species may become extinct in the near future.

The Endangered Species Act

In order to combat this problem, Congress enacted the Endangered Species Act to "conserve to the extent practicable the various species of fish or wildlife and plants facing extinction." They declared their authority to do so pursuant to certain existing international treaties and conventions.

The stated purpose of the Act is "to provide a means whereby the ecosystems upon which endangered species and threatened species depend may be conserved, to provide a program for the conservation of such endangered species and threatened species. . ."

The Act sets forth the procedure to be followed in determining whether a particular species or habitat is endangered or threatened. The Act also calls for the development and implementation of plans for the conservation and survival of listed endangered and threatened species, and sets forth restrictions regarding listed species.

The Act does, however, contain exemptions for the purpose of scientific experimentation pursuant to a permit issued by the Secretary—either the Secretary of the Interior or the Secretary of Commerce depending upon their jurisdiction—under established terms and conditions.

In carrying out its responsibilities under the Endangered Species Act, the United States Fish and Wildlife Service Division of Endangered Species maintains a list of those species determined to be threatened and/or endangered. This listing process is one of the basic functions performed by the Fish and Wildlife Service.

In order to list, reclassify, or delist a species, the USFWS must follow a strict legal process known as a "rulemaking" procedure. The rule is first proposed in the Federal Register, a U.S. government publication. After a public comment period, the USFWS decides if the rule should be approved, revised, or withdrawn.

This process can take up to a year, or longer in unusual circumstances. Participation by all interested parties, including the general public, the scientific community, other government agencies, and foreign governments, is encouraged.

Once an animal or plant is listed, all protective measures authorized by the Endangered Species Act apply to the species and its habitat. Such measures include: (i) protection from any adverse effects of Federal activities; (ii) restrictions on taking, transporting, or selling a species; (iii) authorization for the USFWS to develop and carry out recovery plans; (iv) the authority to purchase important habitat; and (v) Federal aid to State and Commonwealth wildlife agencies that have cooperative agreements with the USFWS.

The USFWS has developed a priority system designed to direct its efforts toward the plants and animals in greatest need of protection. The magnitude of threat is the most important consideration, followed by the immediacy of the threat and the taxonomic distinctiveness of the species. The most distinctive is a monotypic genus, then a full species, and lastly a subspecies, variety, or vertebrate population.

As of 1995, 447 species of animals were listed as threatened and endangered, and 28 species of animals were proposed for listing. 124 species were designated critical habitat; 7 species had proposed critical habitat designations; and 97 species of animals were USFWS candidate species.

More detailed information concerning endangered species and animal rights may be found in this author's legal almanac entitled *Animal Rights*, also published by Oceana Publishing Company.

CHAPTER 8:

ENVIRONMENTAL SELF-AUDIT PRIVILEGE AND IMMUNITY LEGISLATION

In General

The U.S. Environmental Protection Agency defines an environmental audit as a "systematic, documented, periodic and objective review by a regulated entity of facility operations and practices related to meeting environmental requirements." In plain terms, an environmental audit is a method a company uses to evaluate its environmental management system, and its compliance with environmental regulations. Environmental audits are voluntary.

The general thinking behind self-audit privilege and immunity laws is that enforcement authorities should not be focusing enforcement resources on companies that are actively attempting to comply with environmental laws. Many states now recognize that if companies are afraid to conduct environmental audits, then the environment may suffer.

Companies benefit from conducting environmental audits. Environmental compliance audits allow a company to detect and correct violations before regulatory enforcement authorities conduct their inspections. If a problem exists, the company is able to address it early and prevent the problem from becoming a violation. In fact, a company that discloses and corrects an environmental violation discovered through an audit may be immune from punishment, or may receive reduced penalties, depending on the type and extent of the violation.

Environmental audits also project a positive corporate image, demonstrating that the company is responsive to environmental concerns.

A wide variety of companies conduct environmental audits including the (i) aerospace industry; (ii) chemical manufacturers; (iii) construction industry; (iv) utilities and non-utility energy producers; (v) electronics industry; (vi) forestry industry; (vii) mining industry; and (viii) food, alcohol and tobacco industry. This list of industries is not complete. Any company whose operations affect the environment is a candidate for environmental auditing.

State Environmental Self-Audit Privilege and Immunity Legislation

State self-audit privilege laws are designed to provide for the confidentiality of environmental audit results. Some privilege laws prevent only state enforcement authorities from obtaining audit data. Other laws effectively deny enforcement authorities, private plaintiffs, and citizen groups access to audit results.

In addition, state immunity laws reduce or eliminate the liability of companies that disclose and correct violations discovered through an environmental audit. Some state immunity laws guard a company from civil and criminal prosecution. Others offer limited immunity, such as penalty reduction.

Some states have both privilege and immunity legislation. Companies must be aware, however, of any exceptions contained in the law. For example, some states disqualify companies if a court finds that the company conducted an environmental audit for the sole purpose of hiding damaging environmental information.

The self-evaluative privilege, sometimes known as the self-critical analysis privilege, protects documents containing constructive internal criticism from discovery. This privilege allows a company to candidly evaluate its own practices and make beneficial changes.

Federal Environmental Self-Audit Privilege and Immunity Legislation

Presently, under EPA policy, the Department of Justice policy, and the U.S. Sentencing Guidelines, regulated companies who violate environmental regulations receive less favorable treatment than that available under state privilege and immunity legislation.

The EPA's most recent final policy statement offers reduced penalties to regulated entities that voluntarily discover, disclose, and correct environmental violations. The EPA has further stated that it will not recommend the criminal prosecution of a company that voluntarily discovers, discloses, and corrects environmental violations. Nevertheless, repeat offenders, and companies whose violations result in significant harm to human health or the environment, may not qualify for these EPA incentives.

Members of the House and Senate have introduced environmental self-audit privilege and immunity legislation. This bill, however, has not yet become law. The text of the proposed bill, The Voluntary Environmental Self-Evaluation Act, is set forth in the Appendix.

APPENDICES

APPENDIX 1:

TABLE OF ACRONYMS AND ABBREVIATIONS COMMONLY USED IN ENVIRONMENTAL LAW

AAEE: American Academy of Environmental Engineers

AAP: Asbestos Action Program

AAPCO: American Association of Pesticide Control Officials

AARC: Alliance for Acid Rain Control

A&C: Abatement and Control

ACA: American Conservation Association

ACBM: Asbestos-Containing Building Material

ACE: Alliance for Clean Energy

ACEEE: American Council for an Energy Efficient Economy

ACM: Asbestos-Containing Material

ACP: Air Carcinogen Policy

ACQR: Air Quality Control Region

ACTS: Asbestos Contractor Tracking System

ACWA: American Clean Water Association

ACWM: Asbestos-Containing Waste Material

ADABA: Acceptable Data Base

ADSS: Air Data Screening System

AEA: Atomic Energy Act

AEE: Alliance for Environmental Education

AEERL: Air and Energy Engineering Research Laboratory

AEM: Acoustic Emission Monitoring

AERE: Association of Environmental and Resource Economists

AFA: American Forestry Association

AFCA: Area Fuel Consumption Allocation

AFCEE: Air Force Center for Environmental Excellence

AHERA: Asbestos Hazard Emergency Response Act

AID: Agency for International Development

AIHC: American Industrial Health Council

AL: Acceptable Level

APCO: Air Pollution Control Officers

ALARA: As Low As Reasonably Achievable

AMBIENS: Atmospheric Mass Balance of Industrially Emitted and Natural Sulfur

AMOS: Air Management Oversight System

AMPS: Automatic Mapping and Planning System

AMSA: Association of Metropolitan Sewer Agencies

ANC: Acid Neutralizing Capacity

ANPR: Advance Notice of Proposed Rulemaking

ANRHRD: Air, Noise, & Radiation Health Research Division

AOC: Abnormal Operating Conditions

AOD: Argon-Oxygen Decarbonization

AOML: Atlantic Oceanographic and Meteorological Laboratory

APA: Administrative Procedures Act

APCA: Air Pollution Control Association

APCD: Air Pollution Control District

APHA: American Public Health Association

APTI: Air Pollution Training Institute

APWA: American Public Works Association

AQCCT: Air-Quality Criteria and Control Techniques

AQCP: Air Quality Control Program

AQCR: Air-Quality Control Region

AQD: Air-Quality Digest

AQDHS: Air-Quality Data Handling System

AQDM: Air-Quality Display Model

AQMA: Air-Quality Maintenance Area

AQMP: Air-Quality Maintenance Plan

AQMP: Air-Quality Management Plan

AQSM: Air-Quality Simulation Model

AQTAD: Air-Quality Technical Assistance Demonstration

A&R: Air and Radiation

ARAR: Applicable or Relevant and Appropriate Standards, Limitations, Criteria, and Requirements

ARB: Air Resources Board

ARCC: American Rivers Conservation Council

ARCS: Alternative Remedial Contract Strategy

ARG: American Resources Group

ARIP: Accidental Release Information Program

ARL: Air Resources Laboratory

ARM: Air Resources Management

ARO: Alternate Regulatory Option

ARRP: Acid Rain Research Program

ARRPA: Air Resources Regional Pollution Assessment Model

ASDWA: Association of State Drinking Water Administrators

ASHAA: Asbestos in Schools Hazard Abatement Act

ASIWCPA: Association of State and Interstate Water Pollution Control Administrators

AST: Advanced Secondary (Wastewater) Treatment

ASTSWMO: Association of State and Territorial Solid Waste Management Officials

ATERIS: Air Toxics Exposure and Risk Information System

ATS: Action Tracking System

ATSDR: Agency for Toxic Substances and Disease Registry

ATTF: Air Toxics Task Force

A/WPR: Air/Water Pollution Report

AWT: Advanced Wastewater Treatment

AWWA: American Water Works Association

AWWARF: American Water Works Association Research Foundation.

BAC: Biotechnology Advisory Committee

BACM: Best Available Control Measures

BACT: Best Available Control Technology

BADT: Best Available Demonstrated Technology

BaP: Benzo(a)Pyrene

BART: Best Available Retrofit Technology

BAT: Best Available Technology

BATEA: Best Available Treatment Economically Achievable

BCT: Best Control Technology

BCPCT: Best Conventional Pollutant Control Technology

BDAT: Best Demonstrated Achievable Technology

BDCT: Best Demonstrated Control Technology

BDT: Best Demonstrated Technology

BMR: Baseline Monitoring Report

BO: Budget Obligations

BP: Boiling Point

BSI: British Standards Institute

BSO: Benzene Soluble Organics

BTZ: Below the Treatment Zone

BUN: Blood Urea Nitrogen

CA: Citizen Act.

CAA: Clean Air Act

CAAA: Clean Air Act Amendments

CAER: Community Awareness and Emergency Response

CAFO: Consent Agreement/Final Order

CAG: Carcinogenic Assessment Group

CAMP: Continuous Air Monitoring Program

CAO: Corrective Action Order

CAP: Criteria Air Pollutant

CAR: Corrective Action Report

CAS: Center for Automotive Safety

CAS: Chemical Abstract Service

CASAC: Clean Air Scientific Advisory Committee

CAU: Carbon Adsorption Unit

CCAA: Canadian Clean Air Act

CCAP: Center for Clean Air Policy

CD: Climatological Data

CDD: Chlorinated dibenzo-p-dioxin

CDF: Chlorinated dibenzofuran

CDS: Compliance Data System

CEA: Cooperative Enforcement Agreement CEA: Cost and Economic Assessment

CEARC: Canadian Environmental Assessment Research Council

CEB: Chemical Element Balance

CEMS: Continuous Emission Monitoring System

CEPP: Chemical Emergency Preparedness Plan

CEQ: Council on Environmental Quality

CERCLA: Comprehensive Environmental Response, Compensation, and Liability Act (1980)

CERCLIS: Comprehensive Environmental Response, Compensation, and Liability Information System

CERT: Certificate of Eligibility

CFC: Chlorofluorocarbons

CFM: Chlorofluoromethanes

CFR: Code of Federal Regulations

CIS: Chemical Information System.

CLEANS: Clinical Laboratory for Evaluation and Assessment of Toxic Substances

CM: Corrective Measure

CMEP: Critical Mass Energy Project

CNG: Compressed Natural Gas

CPF: Carcinogenic Potency Factor

CPO: Certified Project Officer

CQA: Construction Quality Assurance

CR: Continuous Radon Monitoring

CWA: Clean Water Act (aka FWPCA)

CWAP: Clean Water Action Project

CZMA: Coastal Zone Management Act

DCO: Delayed Compliance Order

DCO: Document Control Officer

DDT: DichloroDiphenylTrichloroethane

DERs: Data Evaluation Records

DES: Diethylstilbesterol

DI: Diagnostic Inspection

DMR: Discharge Monitoring Report

DNA: Deoxyribonucleic acid

DO: Dissolved Oxygen

DPD: Method of measuring chlorine residual in water

DQO: Data Quality Objective

DSAP: Data Self Auditing Program

DSCF: Dry Standard Cubic Feet

DSCM: Dry Standard Cubic Meter

DSS: Domestic Sewage Study

DWEL: Drinking Water Equivalent Level

DWS: Drinking Water Standard

EA: Environmental Audit

EAP: Environmental Action Plan

ECRA: Economic Cleanup Responsibility Act

EDB: Ethylene Dibromide

EDC: Ethylene Dichloride

EDF: Environmental Defense Fund

EDTA: Ethylene Diamine Triacetic Acid

EEA: Energy and Environmental Analysis

EERU: Environmental Emergency Response Unit

EHC: Environmental Health Committee

EHS: Extremely Hazardous Substance

EI: Emissions Inventory

EIA: Environmental Impact Assessment.

EIR: Environmental Impact Report

EIS: Environmental Impact Statement

EL: Exposure Level

ELI: Environmental Law Institute

ELR: Environmental Law Reporter

EM: Electromagnetic Conductivity

EPAA: Environmental Programs Assistance Act

EPCRA: Emergency Preparedness and Community Right to Know Act

ERAMS: Environmental Radiation Ambient Monitoring System

ERC: Emergency Response Commission

ERC: Emissions Reduction Credit

ERC: Environmental Research Center

ERCS: Emergency Response Cleanup Services

ERDA: Energy Research and Development Administration

ERD&DAA: Environmental Research, Development and Demonstration Authorization Act

ERL: Environmental Research Laboratory

ERNS: Emergency Response Notification System

ERT: Emergency Response Team

ERTAQ: ERT Air Quality Model

ES: Enforcement Strategy

ESA: Endangered Species Act

ETS: Environmental Tobacco Smoke

EUP: Experimental Use Permit

ExEx: Expected Exceedance

FACA: Federal Advisory Committee Act

FCC: Fluid Catalytic Converter

FDL: Final Determination Letter

FEDS: Federal Energy Data System

FEPCA: Federal Environmental Pesticide Control Act; enacted as amendments to FIFRA.

FERC: Federal Energy Regulatory Commission

FF: Federal Facilities

FFDCA: Federal Food, Drug, and Cosmetic Act

FIFRA: Federal Insecticide, Fungicide, and Rodenticide Act

FLM: Federal Land Manager

FLPMA: Federal Land Policy and Management Act

FOIA: Freedom Of Information Act

FP: Fine Particulate

FPA: Federal Pesticide Act

FPPA: Federal Pollution Prevention Act

FRA: Federal Register Act

FRN: Final Rulemaking Notice

FS: Feasibility Study

FUA: Fuel Use Act

FURS: Federal Underground Injection Control Reporting System

FWPCA: Federal Water Pollution and Control Act (aka CWA)

GEMS: Global Environmental Monitoring System

GIS: Global Indexing System

GLERL: Great Lakes Environmental Research Laboratory

GPG: Grams-per-Gallon

GPR: Ground-Penetrating Radar

GPS: Groundwater Protection Strategy

GR: Grab Radon Sampling

GWPS: Groundwater Protection Standard

HA: Health Advisory

HAP: Hazardous Air Pollutant

HAPEMS: Hazardous Air Pollutant Enforcement Management System

HC: Hydrocarbon

HCCPD: Hexachlorocyclo-pentadiene

HCP: Hypothermal Coal Process

HDPE: High Density Polyethylene

HEPA: High-Efficiency Particulate Air

HHE: Human Health and the Environment

HI: Hazard Index

HMTA: Hazardous Materials Transportation Act

HRUP: High-Risk Urban Problem

HSDB: Hazardous Substance Data Base

HSL: Hazardous Substance List

HSWA: Hazardous and Solid Waste Amendments

HW: Hazardous Waste

HWM: Hazardous Waste Management

ICBN: International Commission on the Biological Effects of Noise

IES: Institute for Environmental Studies

IP: Inhalable Particles

IPM: Inhalable Particulate Matter

IRM: Intermediate Remedial Measures

JAPCA: Journal of Air Pollution Control Association

LAER: Lowest Achievable Emission Rate

LAMP: Lake Acidification Mitigation Project

LD L0: The lowest dosage of a toxic substance that kills test organisms.

MOE: Margin Of Exposure

MOS: Margin of Safety

MRL: Maximum-Residue Limit

NIOSH: National Institute of Occupational Safety and Health

NSDWR: National Secondary Drinking Water Regulations

OCD: Offshore and Coastal Dispersion

OF: Optional Form

PATS: Pesticide Action Tracking System

PHC: Principal Hazardous Constituent

PHSA: Public Health Service Act

PI: Preliminary Injunction

PIRG: Public Interest Research Group

PM: Particulate Matter

PM10: Particulate Matter (nominally 10m and less)

PM15: Particulate Matter (nominally 15m and less)

PNA: Polynuclear Aromatic Hydrocarbons

PO: Project Officer

POC: Point Of Compliance

POE: Point Of Exposure

POHC: Principal Organic Hazardous Constituent

POI: Point Of Interception

POLREP:Pollution Report

POM: Particulate Organic Matter

POTW: Publicly Owned Treatment Works

PPB: Parts Per Billion

PPIC: Pesticide Programs Information Center

PPT: Parts Per Trillion

PPTH: Parts Per Thousand

PRA: Paperwork Reduction Act

PRA: Planned Regulatory Action

PRP: Potentially Responsible Party

PSC: Program Site Coordinator

PSI: Pounds Per Square Inch

PTFE: Polytetrafluoroethylene (Teflon)

PVC: Polyvinyl Chloride

PWSS: Public Water Supply System

QAC: Quality Assurance Coordinator

QC: Quality Control

QAMIS: Quality Assurance Management and Information System

QCI: Quality Control Index

RA: Reasonable Alternative

RAMS: Regional Air Monitoring System

RAP: Radon Action Program

RAP: Reregistration Assessment Panel

REAP: Regional Enforcement Activities Plan

REE: Rare Earth Elements

REEP: Review of Environmental Effects of Pollutants

REPS: Regional Emissions Projection System

RESOLVE: Center for Environmental Conflict Resolution

RF: Response Factor

RIC: Radon Information Center

RNA: Ribonucleic Acid

RQ: Reportable Quantities

RRC: Regional Response Center

RRT: Regional Response Team

RSD: Risk-Specific Dose

RSE: Removal Site Evaluation

RTECS: Registry of Toxic Effects of Chemical Substances

RUP: Restricted Use Pesticide

S&A: Sampling and Analysis

SAIC: Special-Agents-In-Charge

SAIP: Systems Acquisition and Implementation Program

SANE: Sulfur and Nitrogen Emissions

SARA: Superfund Amendments and Reauthorization Act of 1986

SC: Sierra Club

SCAP: Superfund Consolidated Accomplishments Plan

SCBA: Self-Contained Breathing Apparatus

SCC: Source Classification Code

SCD/SWDC: Soil or Soil and Water Conservation District

SCFM: Standard Cubic Feet Per Minute

SCLDF: Sierra Club Legal Defense Fund

SCRC: Superfund Community Relations Coordinator

SCSA: Soil Conservation Society of America

SCSP: Storm and Combined Sewer Program

SDWA: Safe Drinking Water Act

SEA: State Enforcement Agreement

SEA: State/EPA Agreement

SEP: Standard Evaluation Procedures

SEPWC: Senate Environment and Public Works Committee

SERC: State Emergency Planning Commission

SES: Secondary Emissions Standard

SF: Superfund

SHWL: Seasonal High Water Level

SIP: State Implementation Plan

SITE: Superfund Innovative Technology Evaluation

SOC: Synthetic Organic Chemicals

SPS: State Permit System

SSA: Sole Source Aquifer

SV: Sampling Visit

SWDA: Solid Waste Disposal Act

SWMU: Solid Waste Management Unit

TAMS: Toxic Air Monitoring System

TAMTAC: Toxic Air Monitoring System Advisory Committee

TAPDS: Toxic Air Pollutant Data System

TAS: Tolerance Assessment System

TCDD: Dioxin (Tetrachlorodibenzo-p-dioxin)

THC: Total Hydrocarbons

TOX: Tetradichloroxylene

TPY: Tons Per Year

TQM: Total Quality Management

TSCA: Toxic Substances Control Act

TVA: Tennessee Valley Authority

TWA: Time Weighted Average

TWS: Transient Water System

TZ: Treatment Zone

UAQI: Uniform Air Quality Index

UCC: Ultra Clean Coal

UCL: Upper Control Limit

UEL: Upper Explosive Limit

UFL: Upper Flammability Limit

UIC: Underground Injection Control

UNEP: United Nations Environment Program

USDW: Underground Sources of Drinking Water

USFS: United States Forest Service

UST: Underground Storage Tank

UTP: Urban Transportation Planning

UV: Ultraviolet

UZM: Unsaturated Zone Monitoring

VE: Visual Emissions

VOC: Volatile Organic Compounds

VP: Vapor Pressure

VSD: Virtually Safe Dose

VSS: Volatile Suspended Solids

WAP: Waste Analysis Plan

WCED: World Commission on Environment and Development

WENDB: Water Enforcement National Data Base

WERL: Water Engineering Research Laboratory

WHO: World Health Organization

WHWT: Water and Hazardous Waste Team

WICEM: World Industry Conference on Environmental Management

WL: Warning Letter

WL: Working Level (radon measurement)

WPCF: Water Pollution Control

WQS: Water Quality Standard

WRC: Water Resources Council

WRDA: Water Resources Development Act

WRI: World Resources Institute

WSF: Water Soluble Fraction

WSRA: Wild and Scenic Rivers Act

WSTB: Water Sciences and Technology Board

WSTP: Wastewater Sewage Treatment Plant

WWF: World Wildlife Fund

WWTP: Wastewater Treatment Plant

WWTU: Wastewater Treatment Unit

ZRL: Zero Risk Level

SOURCE: U.S. Environmental Protection Agency

APPENDIX 2:

U.S. ENVIRONMENTAL PROTECTION AGENCY REGIONAL OFFICES

REGION	AREAS COVERED	ADDRESS	TELEPHONE	FAX
Region 1	CT, ME, MA, NH, RI, VT	U.S. EPA - Region 1, John F. Kennedy Federal Building, Boston, MA 02203	(617) 565-3425	(617) 565-3415
Region 2	NJ, NY, PR, VI	U.S. EPA - Region 2, 290 Broadway, New York, NY 10007-1866	(212) 637-3673	(212) 637-4445
Region 3	DE, DC, MD, PA, VA, WV	U.S. EPA - Region 3, 841 Chestnut Building, Philadelphia, PA 19107	(215) 566-3245	(215) 566-5518
Region 4	AL, FL, GA, KY, MS, NC, SC, TN	U.S. EPA - Region 4, 100 Alabama Street, SW, Atlanta,GA 30303	(404) 562-8674	(404) 562-8896
Region 5	IN, MI, MN, OH, WI	U.S. EPA - Region 5, 77 West Jackson Boulevard, Metcalfe Federal Building - 19th Floor, Chicago, IL 60604-3507	(312) 886-6685	(312) 353-1155

REGION	AREAS COVERED	ADDRESS	TELEPHONE	FAX
Region 6	AR, LA, NM, OK, TX	U.S. EPA - Region 6, Tower at Fountain Place, 1445 Ross Avenue,Suite 1200, Dallas, Texas 75202-2733	(214) 665-6617	(214) 665-6660
Region 7	IA, KS, MO, NE	U.S. EPA - Region 7, 726 Minnesota Avenue, Kansas City, KS 66101	(913) 551-7003	(913) 551-7066
Region 8	CO, MT, ND, SD, UT, WY	U.S. EPA - Region 8, 999 18th Street, Suite 500, Denver, CO 80202-2466	(303) 312-6600	(303) 312-7025
Region 9	AZ, CA, HI, NV, AMERICAN SAMOA, GUAM	U.S. EPA - Region 9, 75 Hawthorne Street, San Francisco, CA 94105	(415) 744-2178	(415) 744-1796
Region 10	AK, ID, OR, WA	U.S. EPA - Region 10, 1200 6th Avenue, Seattle, WA 98101	(206) 553-1272	(206) 553-6984

SOURCE: U.S. Environmental Protection Agency

APPENDIX 3:

U.S. ENVIRONMENTAL PROTECTION AGENCY CRIMINAL INVESTIGATION DIVISION - REGIONAL OFFICES

REGION	AREA	ADDRESS	TELEPHONE
REGION I	Boston	U.S. EPA-CID, JFK Federal Building, One Congress Street, Boston, MA 02203-2211	617-565-3636
	New Haven	U.S. EPA-CID, Robert N. Giamo Federal Building, 150 Court Street, Room 433, New Haven, CT 06507-1707	617-565-3436
REGION II	New York	U.S. EPA-CID, 290 Broadway, New York, NY 10007-1866	212-637-3610
	Edison	U.S. EPA-CID, 2890 Woodbridge Avenue, Edison, NJ 08837	908-906-6997
	Buffalo	U.S. EPA-CID, U.S. Attorney's Office, 138 Delaware Avenue, Room 558, Buffalo NY 14202	716-551-4811
REGION III	Philadelphia	U.S. EPA-CID, 841 Chestnut Building, Philadelphia, PA 19107	215-566-2376
	Annapolis	U.S. EPA-CID, 2530 Riva Road, Suite 300, Annapolis, MD 21401	410-573-2784

REGION	AREA	ADDRESS	TELEPHONE
	Pittsburgh/Wheeling	U.S. EPA-CID, Methodist Building, 11th and Chapline Street, Room 109, Wheeling, WV 26003	304-234-0274
REGION IV	Atlanta	U.S. EPA-CID, 100 Alabama Street, Atlanta, GA 30303	404-562-9795
	Charleston	U.S. EPA-CID, P.O. Box 978, Charleston, SC 29402	803-727-4863
	Miami	U.S. EPA-CID, U.S. Attorney's Office, 99 Northeast 4th Street, Room 444, Miami, FL 33132	305-536-3000
	Nashville	U.S. EPA-CID, U.S. Attorney's Office, 450 James Robertson Parkway, Nashville, TN 37243-0485	615-741-3108
REGION V	Chicago	U.S. EPA-CID, 77 West Jackson, Chicago, IL 60604	312-886-9872
	Cleveland	U.S. EPA-CID, 25089 Center Ridge Road, Westlake, OH 44145	216-835-5200
	Detroit	U.S. EPA-CID, 9311 Groh Road, Grosse Ile, MI 48138-1697	313-692-7650
	Minneapolis/St. Paul	U.S. EPA-CID, 316 North Roberts Street, Room 266, St. Paul, MN 55101	612-290-4414

REGION	AREA	ADDRESS	TELEPHONE
	Indianapolis	U.S. EPA-CID, 46 East Ohio Street, 5th Floor, Indianapolis, ID 46204	317-226-5110
REGION VI	Dallas	U.S. EPA-CID, First Interstate Bank at Fountain Place, 1445 Ross Avenue, Suite 1200, Dallas, TX 75202	214-665-6600
	Houston	U.S. EPA-CID, 440 Louisiana, Suite 1150, Houston, TX 77002-1635	713-227-1882
	Baton Rouge	U.S. EPA-CID, 750 Florida Street, Suite 300, Baton Rouge, LA 70821	504-389-0216
REGION VII	St. Louis	U.S. EPA-CID, 1222 Spruce Street, St. Louis, MO 63103	314-539-3422
	Kansas City	U.S. EPA-CID, 726 Minnesota Avenue, Kansas City, KS 66101	913-551-7060
REGION VIII	Denver	U.S. EPA-CID, 999 18th Street, Suite 500, Denver, CO 80202-2466	303-312-6876
REGION IX	San Francisco	U.S. EPA-CID, 75 Hawthorne Street, San Francisco, CA 94105-3901	415-744-2485
	Los Angeles	600 South Lake Avenue, Suite 502, Pasadena, CA 91106	818-583-7528

REGION	AREA	ADDRESS	TELEPHONE
	Phoenix	U.S. EPA-CID, 522 N. Central, Suite 206, Phoenix, AR 85004	602-379-3809
REGION X	Seattle	U.S. EPA-CID, 1200 Six Avenue, Seattle, WA 98101	206-553-8306
	Portland	U.S. EPA-CID, 811 South West 6th Avenue, 3rd Floor, Portland OR 97204	503-326-3541
	Anchorage	U.S. EPA-CID, 222 West 7th Avenue, Suite 19, Anchorage, AK 99513-7588	907-271-6328

SOURCE: U.S. ENVIRONMENTAL PROTECTION AGENCY, CRIMINAL INVES-
TIGATION DIVISION

APPENDIX 4:

U.S. ENVIRONMENTAL PROTECTION AGENCY
DEPARTMENTAL HOTLINES

DEPARTMENT	HOTLINE NUMBER	FAX
Acid Rain Division	202-233-9620	Not supplied
EPA Air Risk Information	919-541-0888	919-541-0824
Asbestos Abatement/Management Ombudsman	800-368-5888	703-305-6462
Office of Air Quality Planning & Standards Control Technology Center	919-541-0800	919-541-0242
Electric and Magnetic Fields (EMF) Information	703-442-8934	703-821-8236
Environmental Financing Information Network (EFIN)	202-564-4994	202-565-2587
Office of Environmental Justice	800-962-6215	202-260-0852
Atmospheric Pollution Prevention Division - Green Lights Program	888-STAR-YES	202-233-9575
Hazardous Waste Ombudsman	800-262-7937	202-260-8929
Indoor Air Quality Information Clearinghouse (IAQINFO)	202-484-1307	Not Supplied
Office of Inspector General - Program Management Division	202-260-4977	202-260-6976
Methods Information Communication Exchange Service (MICE)	703-821-4690	703-448-0282
National Antimicrobial Information Network	800-447-6349	541-737-0761

Methods Information Communication Exchange Service (MICE)	703-821-4690	703-448-0282
National Antimicrobial Information Network	800-447-6349	541-737-0761
National Lead Information Center	800-LEADFYI	202-659-1192
National Pesticide Telecommunications Network	800-858-7378	503-737-0761
National Radon Information	800-SOS-RADON	202-293-0032
National Response Center Hotline	800-424-8802	Not Supplied
National Small Flows Clearinghouse	800-624-8301	304-293-3161
Ozone Protection	800-296-1996	Not Supplied
Pollution Prevention Information Clearinghouse (PPIC)	202-260-1023	202-260-4659
Resource Conservation and Recovery Act/Underground Storage Tank, Superfund and EPCRA	800-424-9346	Not Supplied
Safe Drinking Water Hotline	800-426-4791	703-285-1101
Small Business Ombudsman	800-368-5888	703-305-6462
Stratospheric Ozone Information Hotline	800-296-1996	301-231-6377
Toxic Substances Control Act (TSCA) Assistance Information Service (TAIS)	202-554-1404	202-554-5603
Toxic Release Inventory - User Support Service	202-260-1531	202-401-2347
Wetlands Information Hotline	800-832-7828	703-525-0201

Source: U.S. Environmental Protection Agency

APPENDIX 5:

COMMON AIR POLLUTANTS

POLLUTANT	SOURCE	HEALTH EFFECTS	ENVIRONMENTAL EFFECTS
OZONE	chemical reaction of pollutants; VOCs and NOx	breathing problems, reduced lung function, asthma, irritates eyes, stuffy nose, reduced resistance to colds and other infections, may speed up aging of lung tissue	ozone can damage plants and trees; smog can cause reduced visibility
VOLATILE ORGANIC COMPOUNDS (VOCs)	released from burning fuel, solvents, paints, glues and other products used at work or at home	in addition to ozone effects, many VOCs can cause serious health problems such as cancer	In addition to ozone effects, some VOCs may harm plants
NITROGEN OXIDE	burning of gasoline, natural gas, coal, oil, etc.	lung damage, illnesses of breathing passages and lungs	nitrogen dioxide is an ingredient of acid rain which can damage trees and lakes
CARBON MONOXIDE (CO)	burning of gasoline, natural gas, coal, oil, etc.	reduces ability of blood to bring oxygen to body cells and tissues; cells and tissues need oxygen to work; may be particularly hazardous to people who have heart or circulatory problems and people who have damaged lungs or breathing passages	

POLLUTANT	SOURCE	HEALTH EFFECTS	ENVIRONMENTAL EFFECTS
PARTICULATE MATTER (dust, smoke, soot)	burning of wood, diesel and other fuels; industrial plants; agriculture (plowing, burning off fields); unpaved roads	nose and throat irritation, lung damage, bronchitis, early death	particulates are the main source of haze that reduces visibility
SULFUR DIOXIDE	burning of coal and oil, especially high-sulfur coal from the Eastern United States; industrial processes (paper, metals)	breathing problems, may cause permanent damage to lungs	SO2 is an ingredient in acid rain, which can damage trees and lakes.
LEAD	leaded gasoline; paint,; smelters; manufacture of lead storage batteries	brain and other nervous system damage; children are at special risk; some lead-containing chemicals cause cancer in animals; lead causes digestive and other health problems	lead can harm wildlife.

SOURCE: U.S. ENVIRONMENTAL PROTECTION AGENCY, OFFICE OF AIR QUALITY PLANNING AND STANDARDS

APPENDIX 6:

THE SAFE DRINKING WATER ACT (42 U.S.C. §§300f et seq.)

Section 300f. Definitions

For purposes of this title:

(1) The term "primary drinking water regulation" means a regulation which—

(A) applies to public water systems;

(B) specifies contaminants which, in the judgment of the Administrator, may have any adverse effect on the health of persons;

(C) specifies for each such contaminant either—

(i) a maximum contaminant level, if, in the judgment of the Administrator, it is economically and technologically feasible to ascertain the level of such contaminant in water in public water systems, or

(ii) if, in the judgment of the Administrator, it is not economically or technologically feasible to so ascertain the level of such contaminant, each treatment technique known to the Administrator which leads to a reduction in the level of such contaminant sufficient to satisfy the requirements of section 1412; and

(D) contains criteria and procedures to assure a supply of drinking water which dependably complies with such maximum contaminant levels; including accepted methods for quality control and testing procedures to insure compliance with such levels and to insure proper operation and maintenance of the system, and requirements as to (i) the minimum quality of water which may be taken into the system and (ii) siting for new facilities for public water systems.

At any time after promulgation of a regulation referred to in this paragraph, the Administrator may add equally effective quality control and testing procedures by guidance published in the Federal Register. Such procedures shall be treated as an alternative for public water systems to the quality control and testing procedures listed in the regulation.

(2) The term "secondary drinking water regulation" means a regulation which applies to public water systems and which specifies the maximum contaminant levels which, in the judgment of the Administrator,

are requisite to protect the public welfare. Such regulations may apply to any contaminant in drinking water

(A) which may adversely affect the odor or appearance of such water and consequently may cause a substantial number of the persons served by the public water system providing such water to discontinue its use, or

(B) which may otherwise adversely affect the public welfare. Such regulations may vary according to geographic and other circumstances.

(3) The term "maximum contaminant level" means the maximum permissible level of a contaminant in water which is delivered to any user of a public water system.

(4) Public water system.

(A) In general. The term "public water system" means a system for the provision to the public of water for human consumption through pipes or other constructed conveyances, if such system has at least fifteen service connections or regularly serves at least twenty-five individuals. Such term includes

(i) any collection, treatment, storage, and distribution facilities under control of the operator of such system and used primarily in connection with such system, and

(ii) any collection or pretreatment storage facilities not under such control which are used primarily in connection with such system.

(B) Connections.

(i) In general. For purposes of subparagraph (A), a connection to a system that delivers water by a constructed conveyance other than a pipe shall not be considered a connection, if—

(I) the water is used exclusively for purposes other than residential uses (consisting of drinking, bathing, and cooking, or other similar uses);

(II) the Administrator or the State (in the case of a State exercising primary enforcement responsibility for public water systems) determines that alternative water to achieve the equivalent level of public health protection provided by the applicable national primary drinking water regulation is provided for residential or similar uses for drinking and cooking; or

(III) the Administrator or the State (in the case of a State exercising primary enforcement responsibility for public water systems) determines that the water provided for residential or similar uses for drinking, cooking, and bathing is centrally treated or treated at the point of entry by the provider, a pass-through entity, or the user to achieve the equivalent level of protection provided by the applicable national primary drinking water regulations.

(ii) Irrigation districts. An irrigation district in existence prior to May 18, 1994, that provides primarily agricultural service through a piped water system with only incidental residential or similar use shall not be considered to be a public water system if the system or the residential or similar users of the system comply with subclause (II) or (III) of clause (i).

(C) Transition period. A water supplier that would be a public water system only as a result of modifications made to this paragraph by the Safe Drinking Water Act Amendments of 1996 shall not be considered a public water system for purposes of the Act until the date that is two years after the date of enactment of this subparagraph. If a water supplier does not serve 15 service connections (as defined in subparagraphs (A) and (B)) or 25 people at any time after the conclusion of the 2-year period, the water supplier shall not be considered a public water system.

(5) The term "supplier of water" means any person who owns or operates a public water system.

(6) The term "contaminant" means any physical, chemical, biological, or radiological substance or matter in water.

(7) The term "Administrator" means the Administrator of the Environmental Protection Agency.

(8) The term "Agency" means the Environmental Protection Agency.

(9) The term "Council" means the National Drinking Water Advisory Council established under section 1446.

(10) The term "municipality" means a city, town, or other public body created by or pursuant to State law, or an Indian Tribe.

(11) The term "Federal agency" means any department, agency, or instrumentality of the United States.

(12) The term "person" means an individual, corporation, company, association, partnership, State, municipality, or Federal agency (and in-

cludes officers, employees, and agents of any corporation, company, association, State, municipality, or Federal agency).

(13) (A) Except as provided in subparagraph (B), the term "State" includes, in addition to the several States, only the District of Columbia, Guam, the Commonwealth of Puerto Rico, the Northern Mariana Islands, the Virgin Islands, American Samoa, and the Trust Territory of the Pacific Islands.

(B) For purposes of section 1452, the term "State" means each of the 50 States, the District of Columbia, and the Commonwealth of Puerto Rico.

(14) The term "Indian Tribe" means any Indian tribe having a Federally recognized governing body carrying out substantial governmental duties and powers over any area. For purposes of section 1452, the term includes any Native village (as defined in section 3(c) of the Alaska Native Claims Settlement Act (43 U.S.C. §1602(c))).

(15) Community water system. The term "community water system" means a public water system that—

(A) serves at least 15 service connections used by year-round residents of the area served by the system; or

(B) regularly serves at least 25 year-round residents.

(16) Noncommunity water system. The term "noncommunity water system" means a public water system that is not a community water system.

Section 300g. Coverage

Subject to sections 1415 and 1416, national primary drinking water regulations under this part shall apply to each public water system in each State; except that such regulations shall not apply to a public water system—

(1) which consists only of distribution and storage facilities (and does not have any collection and treatment facilities);

(2) which obtains all of its water from, but is not owned or operated by, a public water system to which such regulations apply;

(3) which does not sell water to any person; and

(4) which is not a carrier which conveys passengers in interstate commerce.

Section 300g-1. National drinking water regulations

(a) National primary drinking water regulations; maximum contaminant level goals; simultaneous publication of regulations and goals.

(1) Effective on the enactment of the Safe Drinking Water Act Amendments of 1986, each national interim or revised primary drinking water regulation promulgated under this section before such enactment shall be deemed to be a national primary drinking water regulation under subsection (b). No such regulation shall be required to comply with the standards set forth in subsection (b)(4) unless such regulation is amended to establish a different maximum contaminant level after the enactment of such amendments.

(2) After the enactment of the Safe Drinking Water Act Amendments of 1986 each recommended maximum contaminant level published before the enactment of such amendments shall be treated as a maximum contaminant level goal.

(3) Whenever a national primary drinking water regulation is proposed under subsection (b) for any contaminant, the maximum contaminant level goal for such contaminant shall be proposed simultaneously. Whenever a national primary drinking water regulation is promulgated under subsection (b) for any contaminant, the maximum contaminant level goal for such contaminant shall be published simultaneously.

(4) Paragraph (3) shall not apply to any recommended maximum contaminant level published before the enactment of the Safe Drinking Water Act Amendments of 1986.

(b) Standards.

(1) Identification of contaminants for listing.

(A) General authority. The Administrator shall, in accordance with the procedures established by this subsection, publish a maximum contaminant level goal and promulgate a national primary drinking water regulation for a contaminant (other than a contaminant referred to in paragraph (2) for which a national primary drinking water regulation has been promulgated as of the date of enactment of the Safe Drinking Water Act Amendments of 1996) if the Administrator determines that—

(i) the contaminant may have an adverse effect on the health of persons;

(ii) the contaminant is known to occur or there is a substantial likelihood that the contaminant will occur in public water systems with a frequency and at levels of public health concern; and

(iii) in the sole judgment of the Administrator, regulation of such contaminant presents a meaningful opportunity for health risk reduction for persons served by public water systems.

(B) Regulation of unregulated contaminants.

(i) Listing of contaminants for consideration.

(I) Not later than 18 months after the date of enactment of the SafeDrinking Water Act Amendments of 1996 and every 5 years thereafter, the Administrator, after consultation with the scientific community, including the Science Advisory Board, after notice and opportunity for public comment, and after considering the occurrence data base established under section 1445(g), shall publish a list of contaminants which, at the time of publication, are not subject to any proposed or promulgated national primary drinking water regulation, which are known or anticipated to occur in public water systems, and which may require regulation under this title.

(II) The unregulated contaminants considered under subclause (I) shall include, but not be limited to, substances referred to in section 101(14) of the Comprehensive Environmental Response, Compensation, and Liability Act of 1980, and substances registered as pesticides under the Federal Insecticide, Fungicide, and Rodenticide Act.

(III) The Administrator's decision whether or not to select an unregulated contaminant for a list under this clause shall not be subject to judicial review.

(ii) Determination to regulate.

(I) Not later than 5 years after the date of enactment of the Safe Drinking Water Act Amendments of 1996, and every 5 years thereafter, the Administrator shall, after notice of the preliminary determination and opportunity for public comment, for not fewer than 5 contaminants included on the list published under clause (i), make determinations of whether or not to regulate such contaminants.

(II) A determination to regulate a contaminant shall be based on findings that the criteria of clauses (i), (ii), and (iii) of subparagraph (A) are satisfied. Such findings shall be based on the best available public health information, including the occurrence data base established under section 1445(g)

(III) The Administrator may make a determination to regulate a contaminant that does not appear on a list under clause (i) if the determination to regulate is made pursuant to subclause (II).

(IV) A determination under this clause not to regulate a contaminant shall be considered final agency action and subject to judicial review.

(iii) Review. Each document setting forth the determination for a contaminant under clause (ii) shall be available for public comment at such time as the determination is published.

(C) Priorities. In selecting unregulated contaminants for consideration under subparagraph (B), the Administrator shall select contaminants that present the greatest public health concern. The Administrator, in making such selection, shall take into consideration, among other factors of public health concern, the effect of such contaminants upon subgroups that comprise a meaningful portion of the general population (such as infants, children, pregnant women, the elderly, individuals with a history of serious illness, or other subpopulations) that are identifiable as being at greater risk of adverse health effects due to exposure to contaminants in drinking water than the general population.

(D) Urgent threats to public health. The Administrator may promulgate an interim national primary drinking water regulation for a contaminant without making a determination for the contaminant under paragraph (4)(C), or completing the analysis under paragraph (3)(C), to address an urgent threat to public health as determined by the Administrator after consultation with and written response to any comments provided by the Secretary of Health and Human Services, acting through the director of the Centers for Disease Control and Prevention or the director of the National Institutes of Health. A determination for any contaminant in accordance with paragraph (4)(C) subject to an interim regulation under this subparagraph shall be issued, and a completed analysis meeting the requirements of paragraph (3)(C) shall be published, not later than 3 years after the date on which the regulation is promulgated and the regulation shall be repromulgated, or revised if appropriate, not later than 5 years after that date.

(E) Regulation. For each contaminant that the Administrator determines to regulate under subparagraph (B), the Administrator shall publish maximum contaminant level goals and promulgate, by rule, national primary drinking water regulations under this subsection. The Administrator shall propose the maximum contaminant level goal and national primary drinking water regulation for a contaminant not later than 24 months after the determination to regulate under subparagraph (B), and may publish such proposed regulation concurrent with the determination to regulate. The Administrator shall publish a maximum contaminant level goal and promulgate a national primary drinking water regulation within 18 months after the proposal thereof. The Administrator, by notice in the Federal Register, may extend the deadline for such promulgation for up to 9 months.

(F) Health advisories and other actions. The Administrator may publish health advisories (which are not regulations) or take other appropriate actions for contaminants not subject to any national primary drinking water regulation.

(2) Schedules and deadlines.

(A) In general. In the case of the contaminants listed in the Advance Notice of Proposed Rulemaking published in volume 47, Federal Register, page 9352, and in volume 48, Federal Register, page 45502, the Administrator shall publish maximum contaminant level goals and promulgate national primary drinking water regulations—

(i) not later than 1 year after June 19, 1986, for not fewer than 9 of the listed contaminants;

(ii) not later than 2 years after June 19, 1986, for not fewer than 40 of the listed contaminants; and

(iii) not later than 3 years after June 19, 1986, for the remainder of the listed contaminants.

(B) Substitution of contaminants. If the Administrator identifies a drinking water contaminant the regulation of which, in the judgment of theAdministrator, is more likely to be protective of public health (taking intoaccount the schedule for regulation under subparagraph (A)) than a contaminant referred to in subparagraph (A), the Administrator may publish a maximum contaminant level goal and promulgate a national primary drinking water regulation for the identified contaminant in lieu of regulating the contaminant referred to in subparagraph (A). Substitutions may be made for not more than 7 contaminants referred to in subparagraph (A). Regulation of a contaminant identified under this subparagraph shall be in accordance with the schedule applicable to the contaminant for which the substitution is made.

(C) Disinfectants and disinfection byproducts. The Administrator shall promulgate an Interim Enhanced Surface Water Treatment Rule, a Final Enhanced Surface Water Treatment Rule, a Stage I Disinfectants and Disinfection Byproducts Rule, and a Stage II Disinfectants and Disinfection Byproducts Rule in accordance with the schedule published in volume 59, Federal Register, page 6361 (February 10, 1994), in table III.13 of the proposed Information Collection Rule. If a delay occurs with respect to the promulgation of any rule in the schedule referred to in this subparagraph, all subsequent rules shall be completed as expeditiously as practicable but no later than a revised date that reflects the interval or intervals for the rules in the schedule.

(3) Risk assessment, management, and communication.

(A) Use of science in decisionmaking. In carrying out this section, and, to the degree that an Agency action is based on science, the Administrator shall use—

(i) the best available, peer-reviewed science and supporting studies conducted in accordance with sound and objective scientific practices; and

(ii) data collected by accepted methods or best available methods (if the reliability of the method and the nature of the decision justifies use of the data).

(B) Public information. In carrying out this section, the Administrator shall ensure that the presentation of information on public health effects is comprehensive, informative, and understandable. The Administrator shall, in a document made available to the public in support of a regulation promulgated under this section, specify, to the extent practicable—

(i) each population addressed by any estimate of public health effects;

(ii) the expected risk or central estimate of risk for the specific populations;

(iii) each appropriate upper-bound or lower-bound estimate of risk;

(iv) each significant uncertainty identified in the process of the assessment of public health effects and studies that would assist in resolving the uncertainty; and

(v) peer-reviewed studies known to the Administrator that support, are directly relevant to, or fail to support any estimate of public health effects and the methodology used to reconcile inconsistencies in the scientific data.

(C) Health risk reduction and cost analysis.

(i) Maximum contaminant levels. When proposing any national primary drinking water regulation that includes a maximum contaminant level, the Administrator shall, with respect to a maximum contaminant level that is being considered in accordance with paragraph (4) and each alternative maximum contaminant level that is being considered pursuant to paragraph (5) or (6)(A), publish, seek public comment on, and use for the purposes of paragraphs (4), (5), and (6) an analysis of each of the following:

(I) Quantifiable and nonquantifiable health risk reduction benefits for which there is a factual basis in the rulemaking record to conclude that such benefits are likely to occur as the result of treatment to comply with each level.

(II) Quantifiable and nonquantifiable health risk reduction benefits for which there is a factual basis in the rulemaking record to conclude that such benefits are likely to occur from reductions in co-occurring contaminants that may be attributed solely to compliance with the maximum contaminant level, excluding benefits resulting from compliance with other proposed or promulgated regulations.

(III) Quantifiable and nonquantifiable costs for which there is a factual basis in the rulemaking record to conclude that such costs are likely to occur solely as a result of compliance with the maximum contaminant level, including monitoring, treatment, and other costs and excluding costs resulting from compliance with other proposed or promulgated regulations.

(IV) The incremental costs and benefits associated with each alternative maximum contaminant level considered.

(V) The effects of the contaminant on the general population and on groups within the general population such as infants, children, pregnant women, the elderly, individuals with a history of serious illness, or other subpopulations that are identified as likely to be at greater risk of adverse health effects due to exposure to contaminants in drinking water than the general population.

(VI) Any increased health risk that may occur as the result of compliance, including risks associated with co-occurring contaminants.

(VII) Other relevant factors, including the quality and extent of the information, the uncertainties in the analysis supporting subclauses (I) through (VI), and factors with respect to the degree and nature of the risk.

(ii) Treatment techniques. When proposing a national primary drinking water regulation that includes a treatment technique in accordance with paragraph (7)(A), the Administrator shall publish and seek public comment on an analysis of the health risk reduction benefits and costs likely to be experienced as the result of compliance with the treatment technique and alternative treatment techniques that are being considered, taking into account, as appropriate, the factors described in clause (i).

(iii) Approaches to measure and value benefits. The Administrator may identify valid approaches for the measurement and valuation of benefits under this subparagraph, including approaches to identify consumer willingness to pay for reductions in health risks from drinking water contaminants.

(iv) Authorization. There are authorized to be appropriated to the Administrator, acting through the Office of Ground Water and Drinking Water, to conduct studies, assessments, and analyses in support of regulations or the development of methods, $35,000,000 for each of fiscal years 1996 through 2003.

(4) Goals and standards.

(A) Maximum contaminant level goals. Each maximum contaminant level goal established under this subsection shall be set at the level at which no known or anticipated adverse effects on the health of persons occur and which allows an adequate margin of safety.

(B) Maximum contaminant levels. Except as provided in paragraphs (5) and (6), each national primary drinking water regulation for a contaminant for which a maximum contaminant level goal is established under this subsection shall specify a maximum contaminant level for such contaminant which is as close to the maximum contaminant level goal as is feasible.

(C) Determination. At the time the Administrator proposes a national primary drinking water regulation under this paragraph, the Administrator shall publish a determination as to whether the benefits of the maximum contaminant level justify, or do not justify, the costs based on the analysis conducted under paragraph (3)(C).

(D) Definition of feasible. For the purposes of this subsection, the term "feasible" means feasible with the use of the best technology, treatment techniques and other means which the Administrator finds, after examination for efficacy under field conditions and not solely under laboratory conditions, are available (taking cost into consideration). For the purpose of this paragraph, granular activated carbon is feasible for the control of synthetic organic chemicals, and any technology, treatment technique, or other means found to be the best available for the control of synthetic organic chemicals must be at least as effective in controlling synthetic organic chemicals as granular activated carbon.

(E) Feasible technologies.

(i) In general. Each national primary drinking water regulation which establishes a maximum contaminant level shall list the technology, treatment techniques, and other means which the Administrator finds to be feasible for purposes of meeting such maximum contaminant level, but a regulation under this subsection shall not require that any specified technology, treatment technique, or other means be used for purposes of meeting such maximum contaminant level.

(ii) List of technologies for small systems. The Administrator shall include in the list any technology, treatment technique, or other means that is affordable, as determined by the Administrator in consultation with the States, for small public water systems serving—

(I) a population of 10,000 or fewer but more than 3,300;

(II) a population of 3,300 or fewer but more than 500; and

(III) a population of 500 or fewer but more than 25; and that achieves compliance with the maximum contaminant level or treatment technique, including packaged or modular systems and point-of-entry or point-of-use treatment units. Point-of-entry and point-of-use treatment units shall be owned, controlled and maintained by the public water system or by a person under contract with the public water system to ensure proper operation and maintenance and compliance with the maximum contaminant level or treatment technique and equipped with mechanical warnings to ensure that customers are automatically notified of operational problems. The Administrator shall not include in the list any point-of-use treatment technology, treatment technique, or other means to achieve compliance with a maximum contaminant level or treatment technique requirement for a microbial contaminant (or an indicator of a microbial contaminant). If the American National Standards Institute has issued product standards applicable to a specific type of point-of-entry or point-of-use treatment unit, individual units of that type shall not be accepted for compliance with a maximum contaminant level or treatment technique requirement unless they are independently certified in accordance with such standards. In listing any technology, treatment technique, or other means pursuant to this clause, the Administrator shall consider the quality of the source water to be treated.

(iii) List of technologies that achieve compliance. Except as provided in clause (v), not later than 2 years after the date of enactment of this clause and after consultation with the States, the Administrator shall issue a list of technologies that achieve compliance with the maximum contaminant level or treatment technique for each category of public water systems described in subclauses (I), (II), and (III) of clause (ii) for each national primary drinking water regulation promulgated prior to the date of enactment of this paragraph.

(iv) Additional technologies. The Administrator may, at any time after a national primary drinking water regulation has been promulgated, supplement the list of technologies describing additional or new or innovative treatment technologies that meet the requirements of this paragraph for categories of small public water systems described in subclauses (I), (II), and (III) of clause (ii) that are subject to the regulation.

(v) Technologies that meet surface water treatment rule. Within one year after the date of enactment of this clause, the Administrator shall list technologies that meet the Surface Water Treatment Rule for each category of public water systems described in subclauses (I), (II), and (III) of clause (ii).

(5) Additional health risk considerations.

(A) In general. Notwithstanding paragraph (4), the Administrator may establish a maximum contaminant level for a contaminant at a level other than the feasible level, if the technology, treatment techniques, and other means used to determine the feasible level would result in an increase in the health risk from drinking water by—

(i) increasing the concentration of other contaminants in drinking water; or

(ii) interfering with the efficacy of drinking water treatment techniques or processes that are used to comply with other national primary drinking water regulations.

(B) Establishment of level. If the Administrator establishes a maximum contaminant level or levels or requires the use of treatment techniques for any contaminant or contaminants pursuant to the authority of this paragraph—

(i) the level or levels or treatment techniques shall minimize the overall risk of adverse health effects by balancing the risk from the contaminant and the risk from other contaminants the concentrations of which may be affected by the use of a treatment technique or process that would be employed to attain the maximum contaminant level or levels; and

(ii) the combination of technology, treatment techniques, or other means required to meet the level or levels shall not be more stringent than is feasible (as defined in paragraph (4)(D)).

(6) Additional health risk reduction and cost considerations.

(A) In general. Notwithstanding paragraph (4), if the Administrator determines based on an analysis conducted under paragraph (3)(C) that the benefits of a maximum contaminant level promulgated in accordance with paragraph (4) would not justify the costs of complying with the level, the Administrator may, after notice and opportunity for public comment, promulgate a maximum contaminant level for the contaminant that maximizes health risk reduction benefits at a cost that is justified by the benefits.

(B) Exception. The Administrator shall not use the authority of this paragraph to promulgate a maximum contaminant level for a contaminant, if the benefits of compliance with a national primary drinking water regulation for the contaminant that would be promulgated in accordance with paragraph (4) experienced by—

(i) persons served by large public water systems; and

(ii) persons served by such other systems as are unlikely, based on information provided by the States, to receive a variance under section 1415(e) (relating to small system variances); would justify the costs to the systems of complying with the regulation. This subparagraph shall not apply if the contaminant is found almost exclusively in small systems eligible under section 1415(e) for a small system variance.

(C) Disinfectants and disinfection byproducts. The Administrator may not use the authority of this paragraph to establish a maximum contaminant level in a Stage I or Stage II national primary drinking water regulation (as described in paragraph (2)(C)) for contaminants that are disinfectants or disinfection byproducts, or to establish a maximum contaminant level or treatment technique requirement for the control of cryptosporidium. The authority of this paragraph may be used to establish regulations for the use of disinfection by systems relying on ground water sources as required by paragraph (8).

(D) Judicial review. A determination by the Administrator that the benefits of a maximum contaminant level or treatment requirement justify or do not justify the costs of complying with the level shall be reviewed by the court pursuant to section 1448 only as part of a review of a final national primary drinking water regulation that has been promulgated based on the determination and shall not be set aside by the court under that section unless the court finds that the determination is arbitrary and capricious.

(7) (A) The Administrator is authorized to promulgate a national primary drinking water regulation that requires the use of a treatment technique in lieu of establishing a maximum contaminant level, if the Administrator makes a finding that it is not economically or technologically feasible to ascertain the level of the contaminant. In such case, the Administrator shall identify those treatment techniques which, in the Administrator's judgment, would prevent known or anticipated adverse effects on the health of persons to the extent feasible. Such regulations

shall specify each treatment technique known to the Administrator which meets the requirements of this paragraph, but the Administrator may grant a variance from any specified treatment technique in accordance with section 1415(a)(3).

(B) Any schedule referred to in this subsection for the promulgation of a national primary drinking water regulation for any contaminant shall apply in the same manner if the regulation requires a treatment technique in lieu of establishing a maximum contaminant level.

(C) (i) Not later than 18 months after the enactment of the Safe Drinking Water Act Amendments of 1986, the Administrator shall propose and promulgate national primary drinking water regulations specifying criteria under which filtration (including coagulation and sedimentation, as appropriate) is required as a treatment technique for public water systems supplied by surface water sources. In promulgating such rules, the Administrator shall consider the quality of source waters, protection afforded by watershed management, treatment practices (such as disinfection and length of water storage) and other factors relevant to protection of health.

(ii) In lieu of the provisions of section 1415 the Administrator shall specify procedures by which the State determines which public water systems within its jurisdiction shall adopt filtration under the criteria of clause (i). The State may require the public water system to provide studies or other information to assist in this determination. The procedures shall provide notice and opportunity for public hearing on this determination. If the State determines that filtration is required, the State shall prescribe a schedule for compliance by the public water system with the filtration requirement. A schedule shall require compliance within 18 months of a determination made under clause (iii).

(iii) Within 18 months from the time that the Administrator establishes the criteria and procedures under this subparagraph, a State with primary enforcement responsibility shall adopt any necessary regulations to implement this subparagraph. Within 12 months of adoption of such regulations the State shall make determinations regarding filtration for all the public water systems within its jurisdiction supplied by surface waters.

(iv) If a State does not have primary enforcement responsibility for public water systems, the Administrator shall have the same authority to make the determination in clause (ii) in such State as the State would have under that clause. Any filtration requirement or schedule under this subparagraph shall be treated as if it were a requirement of a national primary drinking water regulation.

(v) As an additional alternative to the regulations promulgated pursuant to clauses (i) and (iii), including the criteria for avoiding filtration contained in 40 CFR 141.71, a State exercising primary enforcement responsibility for public water systems may, on a case-by-case basis, and after notice and opportunity for public comment, establish treatment requirements as an alternative to filtration in the case of systems having uninhabited, undeveloped watersheds in consolidated ownership, and having control over access to, and activities in, those watersheds, if the State determines (and the Administrator concurs) that the quality of the source water and the alternative treatment requirements established by the State ensure greater removal or inactivation efficiencies of pathogenic organisms for which national primary drinking water regulations have been promulgated or that are of public health concern than would be achieved by the combination of filtration and chlorine disinfection (in compliance with this section).

(8) Disinfection. At any time after the end of the 3-year period that begins on the date of enactment of the Safe Drinking Water Act Amendments of 1996, but not later than the date on which the Administrator promulgates a Stage II rulemaking for disinfectants and disinfection byproducts (as described in paragraph (2)(C)), the Administrator shall also promulgate national primary drinking water regulations requiring disinfection as a treatment technique for all public water systems, including surface water systems and, as necessary, ground water systems. After consultation with the States, the Administrator shall (as part of the regulations) promulgate criteria that the Administrator, or a State that has primary enforcement responsibility under section 1413, shall apply to determine whether disinfection shall be required as a treatment technique for any public water system served by ground water. The Administrator shall simultaneously promulgate a rule specifying criteria that will be used by the Administrator (or delegated State authorities) to grant variances from this requirement according to the provisions of sections 1415(a)(1)(B) and 1415(a)(3). In implementing section 1442(e) the Administrator or the delegated State authority shall, where appropriate, give special consideration to providing technical assistance to small

public water systems in complying with the regulations promulgated under this paragraph.

(9) Review and revision. The Administrator shall, not less often than every 6 years, review and revise, as appropriate, each national primary drinking water regulation promulgated under this title. Any revision of a national primary drinking water regulation shall be promulgated in accordance with this section, except that each revision shall maintain, or provide for greater, protection of the health of persons.

(10) Effective date. A national primary drinking water regulation promulgated under this section (and any amendment thereto) shall take effect on the date that is 3 years after the date on which the regulation is promulgated unless the Administrator determines that an earlier date is practicable, except that the Administrator, or a State (in the case of an individual system), may allow up to 2 additional years to comply with a maximum contaminant level or treatment technique if the Administrator or State (in the case of an individual system) determines that additional time is necessary for capital improvements.

(11) No national primary drinking water regulation may require the addition of any substance for preventive health care purposes unrelated to contamination of drinking water.

(12) Certain contaminants.

(A) Arsenic.

(i) Schedule and standard. Notwithstanding the deadlines set forth in paragraph (1), the Administrator shall promulgate a national primary drinking water regulation for arsenic pursuant to this subsection, in accordance with the schedule established by this paragraph.

(ii) Study plan. Not later than 180 days after the date of enactment of this paragraph, the Administrator shall develop a comprehensive plan for study in support of drinking water rulemaking to reduce the uncertainty in assessing health risks associated with exposure to low levels of arsenic. In conducting such study, the Administrator shall consult with the National Academy of Sciences, other Federal agencies, and interested public and private entities.

(iii) Cooperative agreements. In carrying out the study plan, the Administrator may enter into cooperative agreements with other Federal agencies, State and local governments, and other interested public and private entities.

(iv) Proposed regulations. The Administrator shall propose a national primary drinking water regulation for arsenic not later than January 1, 2000.

(v) Final regulations. Not later than January 1, 2001, after notice and opportunity for public comment, the Administrator shall promulgate a national primary drinking water regulation for arsenic.

(vi) Authorization. There are authorized to be appropriated $2,500,000 for each of fiscal years 1997 through 2000 for the studies required by this paragraph.

(B) Sulfate.

(i) Additional study. Prior to promulgating a national primary drinking water regulation for sulfate, the Administrator and the Director of the Centers for Disease Control and Prevention shall jointly conduct an additional study to establish a reliable dose-response relationship for the adverse human health effects that may result from exposure to sulfate in drinking water, including the health effects that may be experienced by groups within the general population (including infants and travelers) that are potentially at greater risk of adverse health effects as the result of such exposure. The study shall be conducted in consultation with interested States, shall be based on the best available, peer-reviewed science and supporting studies conducted in accordance with sound and objective scientific practices, and shall be completed not later than 30 months after the date of enactment of the Safe Drinking Water ActAmendments of 1996.

(ii) Determination. The Administrator shall include sulfate among the 5 or more contaminants for which a determination is made pursuant to paragraph (3)(B) not later than 5 years after the date of enactment of the Safe Drinking Water Act Amendments of 1996.

(iii) Proposed and final rule. Notwithstanding the deadlines set forth in paragraph (2), the Administrator may, pursuant to the authorities of this subsection and after notice and opportunity for public comment, promulgate a final national primary drinking water regulation for sulfate. Any such regulation shall include requirements for public notification and options for the provision of alternative water supplies to populations at risk as a means of complying with the regulation in lieu of a best available treatment technology or other means.

(13) Radon in drinking water.

(A) National primary drinking water regulation. Notwithstanding paragraph (2), the Administrator shall withdraw any national primary drinking water regulation for radon proposed prior to the date of enactment of this paragraph and shall propose and promulgate a regulation for radon under this section, as amended by the Safe Drinking Water Act Amendments of 1996.

(B) Risk assessment and studies.

(i) Assessment by NAS. Prior to proposing a national primary drinking water regulation for radon, the Administrator shall arrange for the National Academy of Sciences to prepare a risk assessment for radon in drinking water using the best available science in accordance with the requirements of paragraph (3). The risk assessment shall consider each of the risks associated with exposure to radon from drinking water and consider studies on the health effects of radon at levels and under conditions likely to be experienced through residential exposure. The risk assessment shall be peer-reviewed.

(ii) Study of other measures. The Administrator shall arrange for the National Academy of Sciences to prepare an assessment of the health risk reduction benefits associated with various mitigation measures to reduce radon levels in indoor air. The assessment may be conducted as part of the risk assessment authorized by clause (i) and shall be used by the Administrator to prepare the guidance and approve State programs under subparagraph (G).

(iii) Other organization. If the National Academy of Sciences declines to prepare the risk assessment or studies required by this subparagraph, the Administrator shall enter into a contract or cooperative agreement with another independent, scientific organization to prepare such assessments or studies.

(C) Health risk reduction and cost analysis. Not later than 30 months after the date of enactment of this paragraph, the Administrator shall publish, and seek public comment on, a health risk reduction and cost analysis meeting the requirements of paragraph (3)(C) for potential maximum contaminant levels that are being considered for radon in drinking water. The Administrator shall include a response to all significant public comments received on the analysis with the preamble for the proposed rule published under subparagraph (D).

(D) Proposed regulation. Not later than 36 months after the date of enactment of this paragraph, the Administrator shall propose a maximum contaminant level goal and a national primary drinking water regulation for radon pursuant to this section.

(E) Final regulation. Not later than 12 months after the date of the proposal under subparagraph (D), the Administrator shall publish a maximum contaminant level goal and promulgate a national primary drinking water regulation for radon pursuant to this section based on the risk assessment prepared pursuant to subparagraph (B) and the health risk reduction and cost analysis published pursuant to subparagraph (C). In considering the risk assessment and the health risk reduction and cost analysis in connection with the promulgation of such a standard, the Administrator shall take into account the costs and benefits of control programs for radon from other sources.

(F) Alternative maximum contaminant level. If the maximum contaminant level for radon in drinking water promulgated pursuant to subparagraph (E) is more stringent than necessary to reduce the contribution to radon in indoor air from drinking water to a concentration that is equivalent to the national average concentration of radon in outdoor air, the Administrator shall, simultaneously with the promulgation of such level, promulgate an alternative maximum contaminant level for radon that would result in a contribution of radon from drinking water to radon levels in indoor air equivalent to the national average concentration of radon in outdoor air. If the Administrator promulgates an alternative maximum contaminant level under this subparagraph, the Administrator shall, after notice and opportunity for public comment and in consultation with the States, publish guidelines for State programs, including criteria for multimedia measures to mitigate radon levels in indoor air, to be used by the States in preparing programs under subparagraph (G). The guidelines shall take into account data from existing radon mitigation programs and the assessment of mitigation measures prepared under subparagraph (B).

(G) Multimedia radon mitigation programs.

(i) In general. A State may develop and submit a multimedia program to mitigate radon levels in indoor air for approval by the Administrator under this subparagraph. If, after notice and the opportunity for public comment, such program is approved by the Administrator, public water systems in the State may comply with the alternative maximum contaminant level promulgated under subparagraph (F) in lieu of the maximum contaminant level in the national primary drinking water regulation promulgated under subparagraph (E).

(ii) Elements of programs. State programs may rely on a variety of mitigation measures including public education, testing, training, technical assistance, remediation grant and loan or incentive programs, or other regulatory or nonregulatory measures. The effectiveness of elements in State programs shall be evaluated by the Administrator based on the assessment prepared by the National Academy of Sciences under subparagraph (B) and the guidelines published by the Administrator under subparagraph (F).

(iii) Approval. The Administrator shall approve a State program submitted under this paragraph if the health risk reduction benefits expected to be achieved by the program are equal to or greater than the health risk reduction benefits that would be achieved if each public water system in the State complied with the maximum contaminant level promulgated under subparagraph (E). The Administrator shall approve or disapprove a program submitted under this paragraph within 180 days of receipt. A program that is not disapproved during such period shall be deemed approved. A program that is disapproved may be modified to address the objections of the Administrator and be resubmitted for approval.

(iv) Review. The Administrator shall periodically, but not less often than every 5 years, review each multimedia mitigation program approved under this subparagraph to determine whether it continues to meet the requirements of clause (iii) and shall, after written notice to the State and an opportunity for the State to correct any deficiency in the program, withdraw approval of programs that no longer comply with such requirements.

(v) Extension. If, within 90 days after the promulgation of an alternative maximum contaminant level under subparagraph (F), the Governor of a State submits a letter to the Administrator committing to develop a multimedia mitigation program under this subparagraph, the effective date of the national primary drinking water regulation for radon in the State that would be applicable under paragraph (10) shall be extended for a period of 18 months.

(vi) Local programs. In the event that a State chooses not to submit a multimedia mitigation program for approval under this subparagraph or has submitted a program that has been disapproved, any public water system in the State may submit a program for approval by the Administrator according to the same criteria, conditions, and approval process that would apply to a State program. The Administrator shall approve a multimedia mitigation program if the health risk reduction benefits expected to be achieved by the program are equal to or greater than the health risk reduction benefits that would result from compliance by the public water system with the maximum contaminant level for radon promulgated under subparagraph (E).

(14) Recycling of filter backwash. The Administrator shall promulgate a regulation to govern the recycling of filter backwash water within the treatment process of a public water system. The Administrator shall promulgate such regulation not later than 4 years after the date of enactment of the Safe Drinking Water Act Amendments of 1996, unless such recycling has been addressed by the Administrator's Enhanced Surface Water Treatment Rule prior to such date.

(15) Variance technologies.

(A) In general. At the same time as the Administrator promulgates a national primary drinking water regulation for a contaminant pursuant to this section, the Administrator shall issue guidance or regulations describing the best treatment technologies, treatment techniques, or other means (referred to in this paragraph as "variance technology") for the contaminant that the Administrator finds, after examination for efficacy under field conditions and not solely under laboratory conditions, are available and affordable, as determined by the Administrator in consultation with the States, for public water systems of varying size, considering the quality of the source water to be treated. The Administrator shall identify such variance technologies for public water systems serving—

(i) a population of 10,000 or fewer but more than 3,300;

(ii) a population of 3,300 or fewer but more than 500; and

(iii) a population of 500 or fewer but more than 25, if, considering the quality of the source water to be treated, no treatment technology is listed for public water systems of that size under paragraph (4)(E). Variance technologies identified by the Administrator pursuant to this paragraph may not achieve compliance with the maximum contaminant level or treatment technique requirement of such regulation, but shall achieve the maximum reduction or inactivation efficiency that is affordable considering the size of the system and the quality of the source water. The guidance or regulations shall not require the use of a technology from a specific manufacturer or brand.

(B) Limitation. The Administrator shall not identify any variance technology under this paragraph, unless the Administrator has determined, considering the quality of the source water to be treated and the expected useful life of the technology, that the variance technology is protective of public health.

(C) Additional information. The Administrator shall include in the guidance or regulations identifying variance technologies under this paragraph any assumptions supporting the public health determination referred to in subparagraph (B), where such assumptions concern the public water system to which the technology may be applied, or its source waters. The Administrator shall provide any assumptions used in determining affordability, taking into consideration the number of persons served by such systems. The Administrator shall provide as much reliable information as practicable on performance, effectiveness, limitations, costs, and other relevant factors including the applicability of variance technology to waters from surface and underground sources.

(D) Regulations and guidance. Not later than 2 years after the date of enactment of this paragraph and after consultation with the States, the Administrator shall issue guidance or regulations under subparagraph (A) for each national primary drinking water regulation promulgated prior to the date of enactment of this paragraph for which a variance may be granted under section 1415(e). The Administrator may, at any time after a national primary drinking water regulation has been promulgated, issue guidance or regulations describing additional variance technologies. The Administrator shall, not less often than every 7 years, or upon receipt of a petition supported by substantial information, review variance technologies identified under this paragraph. The Administrator shall issue revised guidance or regulations if new or innovative variance technologies become available that meet the requirements of this paragraph and achieve an equal or greater reduction or inactivation efficiency than the variance technologies previously identified under this subparagraph. No public water system shall be required to replace a variance technology during the useful life of the technology for the sole reason that a more efficient variance technology has been listed under this subparagraph.

(c) Secondary regulations; publication of proposed regulations; promulgation; amendments. The Administrator shall publish proposed national secondary drinking water regulations within 270 days after the date of enactment of this title. Within 90 days after publication of any such regulation, he shall promulgate such regulation with such modifications as he deems appropriate. Regulations under this subsection may be amended from time to time.

(d) Regulations; public hearings; administrative consultations. Regulations under this section shall be prescribed in accordance with section 553 of title 5, United States Code (relating to rule-making), except that the Administrator shall provide opportunity for public hearing prior to promulgation of such regulations. In proposing and promulgating regulations under this section, the Administrator shall consult with the Secretary and the National Drinking Water Advisory Council.

(e) Science Advisory Board comments. The Administrator shall request comments from the Science Advisory Board (established under the Environmental Research, Development, and Demonstration Act of 1978) prior to proposal of a maximum contaminant level goal and national primary drinking water regulation. The Board shall respond, as it deems appropriate, within the time period applicable for promulgation of the national primary drinking water standard concerned. This subsection shall, under no circumstances, be used to delay final promulgation of any national primary drinking water standard.

Section 300i-1. Tampering with public water systems

(a) Tampering. Any person who tampers with a public water system shall be imprisoned for not more than 5 years, or fined in accordance with title 18 of the United States Code, or both.

(b) Attempt or threat. Any person who attempts to tamper, or makes a threat to tamper, with a public drinking water system be imprisoned for not more than 3 years, or fined in accordance with title 18 of the United States Code, or both.

(c) Civil penalty. The Administrator may bring a civil action in the appropriate United States district court (as determined under the provisions of title 28 of the United States Code) against any person who tampers, attempts to tamper, or makes a threat to tamper with a public water system. The court may impose on such person a civil penalty of not more than $ 50,000 for such tampering or not more than $ 20,000 for such attempt or threat.

(d) "Tamper" defined. For purposes of this section, the term "tamper" means—

(1) to introduce a contaminant into a public water system with the intention of harming persons; or

(2) to otherwise interfere with the operation of a public water system with the intention of harming persons.

Section 300j-5. National Drinking Water Advisory Council

(a) Establishment; membership; representation of interests; term of office, vacancies; reappointment. There is established a National Drink Water Advisory Council which shall consist of fifteen members appointed by the Administrator after consultation with the Secretary. Five members shall be appointed from the general public; five members shall be appointed from appropriate State and local agencies concerned with water hygiene and public water supply; and five members shall be appointed from representatives of private organizations or groups demonstrating an active interest in the field of water hygiene and public water supply, of which two such members shall be associated with small, rural public water systems. Each member of the Council shall hold office for a term of three years, except that—

(1) any member appointed to fill a vacancy occurring prior to the expiration of the term for which his predecessor was appointed shall be appointed for the remainder of such term; and

(2) the terms of the members first taking office shall expire as follows: Five shall expire three years after the date of enactment of this title, five shall expire two years after such date, and five shall expire one year after such date, as designated by the Administrator at the time of appointment. The members of the Council shall be eligible for reappointment.

(b) Functions. The Council shall advise, consult with, and make recommendations to, the Administrator on matters relating to activities, functions, and policies of the Agency under this title.

(c) Compensation and allowances; travel expenses. Members of the Council appointed under this section shall, while attending meetings or conferences of the Council or otherwise engaged in business of the Council, receive compensation and allowances at a rate to be fixed by the

Administrator, but not exceeding the daily equivalent of the annual rate of basic pay in effect for grade GS-18 of the General Schedule for each day (including traveltime) during which they are engaged in the actual performance of duties vested in the Council. While away from their homes or regular places of business in the performance of services for the Council, members of the Council shall be allowed travel expenses, including per diem in lieu of subsistence, in the same manner as persons employed intermittently in the Government service are allowed expenses under section 5703(b) of title 5 of the United States Code.

(d) Advisory committee termination provision inapplicable. Section 14(a) of the Federal Advisory Committee Act (relating to termination) [5 USCS Appx. §14(a)] shall not apply to the Council.

Section 300j-6. Federal agencies

(a) In general. Each department, agency, and instrumentality of the executive, legislative, and judicial branches of the Federal Government—

(1) owning or operating any facility in a wellhead protection area;

(2) engaged in any activity at such facility resulting, or which may result, in the contamination of water supplies in any such area;

(3) owning or operating any public water system; or

(4) engaged in any activity resulting, or which may result in, underground injection which endangers drinking water (within the meaning of section 1421(d)(2), shall be subject to, and comply with, all Federal, State, interstate, and local requirements, both substantive and procedural (including any requirement for permits or reporting or any provisions for injunctive relief and such sanctions as may be imposed by a court to enforce such relief), respecting the protection of such wellhead areas, respecting such public water systems, and respecting any underground injection in the same manner and to the same extent as any person is subject to such requirements, including the payment of reasonable service charges. The Federal, State, interstate, and local substantive and procedural requirements referred to in this subsection include, but are not limited to, all administrative orders and all civil and administrative penalties and fines, regardless of whether such penalties or fines are punitive or coercive in nature or are imposed for isolated, intermittent, or continuing violations. The United States hereby expressly waives any immunity otherwise applicable to the United States with respect to any such substantive or procedural requirement (including, but not limited to, any injunctive relief, administrative order or civil or administrative penalty or

fine referred to in the preceding sentence, or reasonable service charge). The reasonable service charges referred to in this subsection include, but are not limited to, fees or charges assessed in connection with the processing and issuance of permits, renewal of permits, amendments to permits, review of plans, studies, and other documents, and inspection and monitoring of facilities, as well as any other nondiscriminatory charges that are assessed in connection with a Federal, State, interstate, or local regulatory program respecting the protection of wellhead areas or public water systems or respecting any underground injection. Neither the United States, nor any agent, employee, or officer thereof, shall be immune or exempt from any process or sanction of any State or Federal Court with respect to the enforcement of any such injunctive relief. No agent, employee, or officer of the United States shall be personally liable for any civil penalty under any Federal, State, interstate, or local law concerning the protection of wellhead areas or public water systems or concerning underground injection with respect to any act or omission within the scope of the official duties of the agent, employee, or officer. An agent, employee, or officer of the United States shall be subject to any criminal sanction (including, but not limited to, any fine or imprisonment) under any Federal or State requirement adopted pursuant to this title, but no department, agency, or instrumentality of the executive, legislative, or judicial branch of the Federal Government shall be subject to any such sanction. The President may exempt any facility of any department, agency, or instrumentality in the executive branch from compliance with such a requirement if he determines it to be in the paramount interest of the United States to do so. No such exemption shall be granted due to lack of appropriation unless the President shall have specifically requested such appropriation as a part of the budgetary process and the Congress shall have failed to make available such requested appropriation. Any exemption shall be for a period not in excess of 1 year, but additional exemptions may be granted for periods not to exceed 1 year upon the President's making a new determination. The President shall report each January to the Congress all exemptions from the requirements of this section granted during the preceding calendar year, together with his reason for granting each such exemption.

(b) Administrative penalty orders.

(1) In general. If the Administrator finds that a Federal agency has violated an applicable requirement under this title, the Administrator may issue a penalty order assessing a penalty against the Federal agency.

(2) Penalties. The Administrator may, after notice to the agency, assess a civil penalty against the agency in an amount not to exceed $25,000 per day per violation.

(3) Procedure. Before an administrative penalty order issued under this subsection becomes final, the Administrator shall provide the agency an opportunity to confer with the Administrator and shall provide the agency notice and an opportunity for a hearing on the record in accordance with chapters 5 and 7 of title 5, United States Code.

(4) Public review.

(A) In general. Any interested person may obtain review of an administrative penalty order issued under this subsection. The review may be obtained in the United States District Court for the District of Columbia or in the United States District Court for the district in which the violation is alleged to have occurred by the filing of a complaint with the court within the 30-day period beginning on the date the penalty order becomes final. The person filing the complaint shall simultaneously send a copy of the complaint by certified mail to the Administrator and the Attorney General.

(B) Record. The Administrator shall promptly file in the court a certified copy of the record on which the order was issued.

(C) Standard of review. The court shall not set aside or remand the order unless the court finds that there is not substantial evidence in the record, taken as a whole, to support the finding of a violation or that the assessment of the penalty by the Administrator constitutes an abuse of discretion.

(D) Prohibition on additional penalties. The court may not impose an additional civil penalty for a violation that is subject to the order unless the court finds that the assessment constitutes an abuse of discretion by the Administrator.

(c) Limitation on State use of funds collected from Federal Government. Unless a State law in effect on the date of enactment of the Safe Drinking Water Act Amendments of 1996 or a State constitution requires the funds to be used in a different manner, all funds collected by a State from the Federal Government from penalties and fines imposed for violation of any substantive or procedural requirement referred to in subsection (a) shall be used by the State only for projects designed to improve or protect the environment or to defray the costs of environmental protection or enforcement.

(d) Indian rights and sovereignty as unaffected; "Federal agency" defined.

(1) Nothing in the Safe Drinking Water Amendments of 1977 shall be construed to alter or affect the status of American Indian lands or water rights nor to waive any sovereignty over Indian lands guaranteed by treaty or statute.

(2) For the purposes of this Act, the term "Federal agency" shall not be construed to refer to or include any American Indian tribe, nor to the Secretary of the Interior in his capacity as trustee of Indian lands.

(e) Washington Aqueduct. The Secretary of the Army shall not pass the cost of any penalty assessed under this title on to any customer, user, or other purchaser of drinking water from the Washington Aqueduct system, including finished water from the Dalecarlia or McMillan treatment plant.

Section 300j-7. Judicial review

(a) Courts of appeals; petition for review: actions respecting regulations; filing period; grounds arising after expiration of filing period; exclusiveness of remedy. A petition for review of—

(1) actions pertaining to the establishment of national primary drinking water regulations (including maximum contaminant level goals) may be filed only in the United States Court of Appeals for the District of Columbia circuit; and

(2) any other final action of the Administrator under this Act may be filed in the circuit in which the petitioner resides or transacts business which is directly affected by the action.

Any such petition shall be filed within the 45-day period beginning on the date of the promulgation of the regulation or any final Agency action with respect to which review is sought or on the date of the determination with respect to which review is sought, and may be filed after the expiration of such 45-day period if the petition is based solely on grounds arising after the expiration of such period. Action of the Administrator with respect to which review could have been obtained under this subsection shall not be subject to judicial review in any civil or criminal proceeding for enforcement or in any civil action to enjoin enforcement. In any petition concerning the assessment of a civil penalty pursuant to section 1414(g)(3)(B), the petitioner shall simultaneously send a copy of the complaint by certified mail to the Administrator and the Attorney General. The court shall set aside and remand the penalty order if the court finds that there is not substantial evidence in the record to support the finding of a violation or that the assessment of the penalty by the Administrator constitutes an abuse of discretion.

(b) District courts; petition for review: actions respecting variances or exemptions; filing period; grounds arising after expiration of filing period; exclusiveness of remedy. The United States district courts shall have jurisdiction of actions brought to review (1) the granting of, or the refusing to grant, a variance or exemption under section 1415 or 1416 or (2) the requirements of any schedule prescribed for a variance or exemption under such section or the failure to prescribe such a schedule. Such an action may only be brought upon a petition for review filed with the court within the 45-day period beginning on the date the action sought to be reviewed is taken or, in the case of a petition to review the refusal to grant a variance or exemption or the failure to prescribe a schedule, within the 45-day period beginning on the date action is required to be taken on the variance, exemption, or schedule, as the case may be. A petition for such review may be filed after the expiration of such period if the petition is based solely on grounds arising after the expiration of such period. Action with respect to which review could have been obtained under this subsection shall not be subject to judicial review in any civil or criminal proceeding for enforcement or in any civil action to enjoin enforcement.

(c) Judicial order for additional evidence before Administrator; modified or new findings; recommendation for modification or setting aside of original determination. In any judicial proceeding in which review is sought of a determination under this title required to be made on the record after notice and opportunity for hearing, if any party applies to the court for leave to adduce additional evidence and shows to the satisfaction of the court that such additional evidence is material and that there were reasonable grounds for the failure to adduce such evidence in the proceeding before the Administrator, the court may order such additional evidence (and evidence in rebuttal thereof) to be taken before the Administrator, in such manner and upon such terms and conditions as the court may deem proper. The Administrator may modify his findings as to the facts, or make new findings, by reason of the additional evidence so taken, and he shall file such modified or new findings, and his recommendation, if any, for the modification or setting aside of his original determination, with the return of such additional evidence.

300j-8. Citizen's civil actions

(a) Persons subject to civil actions; jurisdiction of enforcement proceedings. Except as provided in subsection (b) of this section, any person may commence a civil action on his own behalf—

(1) against any person (including (A) the United States, and (B) any other governmental instrumentality or agency to the extent permitted by the eleventh amendment to the Constitution) who is alleged to be in violation of any requirement prescribed by or under this title;

(2) against the Administrator where there is alleged a failure of the Administrator to perform any act or duty under this title which is not discretionary with the Administrator; or

(3) for the collection of a penalty by the United States Government (and associated costs and interest) against any Federal agency that fails, by the date that is 18 months after the effective date of a final order to pay a penalty assessed by the Administrator under section 1429(b), to pay the penalty.

No action may be brought under paragraph (1) against a public water system for a violation of a requirement prescribed by or under this title which occurred within the 27-month period beginning on the first day of the month in which this title is enacted. The United States district courts shall have jurisdiction, without regard to the amount in controversy or the citizenship of the parties, to enforce in an action brought under this subsection any requirement prescribed by or under this title or to order the Administrator to perform an act or duty described in paragraph (2), as the case may be.

(b) Conditions for commencement of civil action; notice. No civil action may be commenced—

(1) under subsection (a)(1) of this section respecting violation of a requirement prescribed by or under this title—

(A) prior to sixty days after the plaintiff has given notice of such violation (i) to the Administrator, (ii) to any alleged violator of such requirement and (iii) to the State in which the violation occurs, or

(B) if the Administrator, the Attorney General, or the State has commenced and is diligently prosecuting a civil action in a court of the United States to require compliance with such requirement, but in any such action in a court of the United States any person may intervene as a matter of right; or (2) under subsection (a)(2) of this section prior to sixty days after the plaintiff has given notice of such action to the Administrator; or (3) under subsection (a)(3) prior to 60 days after the plaintiff has given notice of such action to the Attorney General and to the Federal agency.

Notice required by this subsection shall be given in such manner as the Administrator shall prescribe by regulation. No person may commence a civil action under subsection (a) to require a State to prescribe a schedule under section 1415 or 1416 for a variance or exemption, unless such person shows to the satisfaction of the court that the State has in a substantial number of cases failed to prescribe such schedules.

(c) Intervention of right. In any action under this section, the Administrator or the Attorney General, if not a party, may intervene as a matter of right.

(d) Costs; attorney fees; expert witness fees; filing of bond. The court, in issuing any final order in any action brought under subsection (a) of this section, may award costs of litigation (including reasonable attorney and expert witness fees) to any party whenever the court determines such an award is appropriate. The court may, if a temporary restraining order or preliminary injunction is sought, require the filing of a bond or equivalent security in accordance with the Federal Rules of Civil Procedure.

(e) Availability of other relief. Nothing in this section shall restrict any right which any person (or class of persons) may have under any statute or common law to seek enforcement of any requirement prescribed by or under this title or to seek any other relief. Nothing in this section or in any other law of the United States shall be construed to prohibit, exclude, or restrict any State or local government from—

(1) bringing any action or obtaining any remedy or sanction in any State or local court, or

(2) bringing any administrative action or obtaining any administrative remedy or sanction, against any agency of the United States under State or local law to enforce any requirement respecting the provision of safe drinking water or respecting any underground injection control program. Nothing in this section shall be construed to authorize judicial review of regulations or orders of the Administrator under this title, except as provided in section 1448. For provisions providing for application of certain requirements to such agencies in the same manner as to nongovernmental entities, see section 1447.

APPENDIX 7:

U.S. ENVIRONMENTAL PROTECTION AGENCY
WETLANDS DIVISION - REGIONAL OFFICES

REGION	AREAS COVERED	ADDRESS	TELEPHONE	FAX
Headquarters	Overall	U.S. EPA - Wetlands Division, 401 M Street SW, Washington, DC 20460	(202) 260-7791	(202) 260-2356
Region I	CT, MA, ME, MH, RI, VT	U.S. EPA - Wetlands Division - Region I, John F. Kennedy Federal Building, Boston, MA 02203-1911	(617) 565-4421	(617) 565-4940
Region II	NJ, NY, PR, VI	U.S. EPA - Wetlands Division - Region II, 26 Federal Plaza, Room 837, New York, NY 10278	(212) 264-5170	(212) 264-4690
Region III	DE, MD, PA, VA, WV	U.S. EPA - Wetlands Division - Region III, 841 Chestnut Street, Philadelphia, PA 19107	(215) 597-9301	(215) 597-1850

REGION	AREAS COVERED	ADDRESS	TELEPHONE	FAX
Region IV	AL, FL, GA, KY, MS, NC, SC, TN	U.S. EPA - Wetlands Division - Region IV, 345 Courtland Street, N.E., Atlanta, GA 30365	(404) 347-4015	(404) 347-3269
Region V	IL, IN, MI, MN, OH, WI	U.S. EPA - Wetlands Division - Region V, 77 West Jackson Boulevard, Chicago, IL 60604	(312) 886-0243	(312) 886-7804
Region VI	AR, LA, NM, OK, TX	U.S. EPA - Wetlands Division - Region VI, 1445 Ross Avenue, Suite 900, Dallas, TX 75202	(214) 655-2263	(214) 655-7446
Region VII	IA, KS, MO, NE	U.S. EPA - Wetlands Division - Region VII, 726 Minnesota Avenue, Kansas City, KS 66101	(913) 551-7540	(913) 551-7863
Region VIII	CO, MT, ND, SD, UT, WY	U.S. EPA - Wetlands Division - Region VIII, 999 18th Street, 500 Denver Place, Denver, CO 80202-2405	(303) 293-1570	(303) 391-6957

REGION	AREAS COVERED	ADDRESS	TELEPHONE	FAX
Region IX	AZ, CA, HI, NV, Pacific Islands	U.S. EPA - Wetlands Division - Region IX, 75 Hawthorne Street, San Francisco, CA 94105	(415) 744-1968	(415) 744-1078
Region X	AK, ID, OR, WA	U.S. EPA - Wetlands Division - Region X, 1200 Sixth Avenue, Seattle, WA 98101	(206) 553-1412	(206) 553-1775

SOURCE: U.S. Environmental Protection Agency, Wetlands Division

THE VOLUNTARY ENVIRONMENTAL SELF-EVALUATION ACT

HR 1047 IH - 104th CONGRESS - 1st Session

Background: Introduced on February 24, 1995 to the House of Representatives by Mr. Hefley, Mr. Hyde, Mr. Schaefer, Mr. Crapo, Mr. Allard, Mr. Delay and Mr. Young. Referred to the Committee on the Judiciary and, in addition, to the Committees on Commerce, Transportation and Infrastructure, and Agriculture, for a period to be subsequently determined by the Speaker, in each case for consideration of such provisions as fall within the jurisdiction of the committee concerned

A BILL

To provide under Federal law a limited privilege from disclosure of certain information acquired pursuant to a voluntary environmental self-evaluation and, if such information is voluntarily disclosed, for limited immunity from penalties.

Be it enacted by the Senate and House of Representatives of the United States of America in Congress assembled,

SECTION 1. SHORT TITLE.

This Act may be cited as the Voluntary Environmental Self-Evaluation Act.

SECTION 2. FINDINGS.

Congress finds that—

(1) enhanced and efficient protection of public health and welfare under Federal environmental laws depends principally on voluntary compliance by the general public, rather than enforcement;

(2) both a limited privilege from disclosure and a limited expansion of the protection of members of the general public who voluntarily disclose information as a result of a voluntary environmental self-evaluation is necessary to encourage voluntary compliance with Federal environmental laws and to protect public health and welfare; and

(3) the protection referred to in paragraph (2) will not inhibit the carrying out of regulatory authority that is mandatory under Federal envi-

ronmental laws by officials who are entrusted with the duty of protecting the environment of the United States.

SECTION 3. DEFINITIONS.

As used in this Act:

(1) ADMINISTRATOR- The term "Administrator" means the Administrator of the Environmental Protection Agency.

(2) ENTITY- The term "entity" means a unit of State or local government.

(3) FEDERAL AGENCY- The term "Federal agency" has the meaning provided the term "agency" under section 551 of title 5, United States Code.

(4) FEDERAL ENVIRONMENTAL LAW- The term "Federal environmental law"—

(A) means—

(i) the Federal Insecticide, Fungicide, and Rodenticide Act (7 U.S.C. 136 et seq.);

(ii) the Toxic Substances Control Act (15 U.S.C. 2601 et seq.);

(iii) the Federal Water Pollution Control Act (33 U.S.C. 1251 et seq.);

(iv) title XIV of the Public Health Service Act (commonly known as the "Safe Drinking Water Act") (42 U.S.C. 300f et seq.);

(v) the Solid Waste Disposal Act (42 U.S.C. 6901 et seq.);

(vi) the Clean Air Act (42 U.S.C. 7401 et seq.);

(vii) the Comprehensive Environmental Response, Compensation, and Liability Act of 1980 (42 U.S.C. 9601 et seq.);

(viii) the Emergency Planning and Community Right-To-Know Act of 1986 (42 U.S.C. 11001 et seq.);

(ix) the Oil Pollution Act of 1990 (33 U.S.C. 2701 et seq.);

(x) the Noise Control Act of 1982 (42 U.S.C. 4901 et seq.); and

(xi) the Pollution Prevention Act of 1990 (42 U.S.C. 13101 et seq.);

(B) includes any regulation issued under a law listed in subparagraph (A); and

(C) includes the terms and conditions of any permit issued under a law listed in subparagraph (A).

(5) VOLUNTARY DISCLOSURE- The term "voluntary disclosure" means the disclosure of information related to a voluntary environmental self-evaluation with respect to which the protections provided under this Act apply.

(6) VOLUNTARY ENVIRONMENTAL SELF-EVALUATION- The term"voluntary environmental self-evaluation" means an assessment, audit, investigation or review that is—

(A) initiated by a person or entity;

(B) carried out by the person or entity, or a consultant employed by the person or entity, for the express purpose of carrying out the assessment, audit, or review; and

(C) carried out to determine whether the person or entity is in compliance with Federal environmental laws (including any permit issued under a Federal environmental law).

SECTION 4. ADMISSIBILITY OF REPORTS, FINDINGS, OPINIONS, OR OTHER COMMUNICATIONS.

(a) IN GENERAL- Subject to subsection (b) and notwithstanding any other provision of law, a report, finding, opinion, or other communication of a person or entity related to, and essentially constituting a part of, a voluntary environmental self-evaluation that is made in good faith shall not be admissible evidence in any legal action or administrative procedure under Federal law and shall not be subject to any discovery procedure under Federal law, unless—

(1) the person or entity that initiated the self-evaluation expressly waives the right of the person or entity to exclude from the evidence or procedure material subject to this section; or

(2) after an in camera hearing, the appropriate Federal court determines that—

(A)(i) the report, finding, opinion, or other communication indicates noncompliance with a Federal environmental law; and

(ii) the person or entity failed to initiate efforts to achieve compliance with the law within a period of time that is reasonable and that is adequate to achieve compliance (including submitting an appropriate permit application);

(B) compelling circumstances—

(i) make it necessary to admit the environmental audit report, finding, opinion, or other communication into evidence; or

(ii) necessitate that the environmental audit report, finding, opinion, or other communication be subject to discovery procedures;

(C) the person or entity is asserting the applicability of the exclusion under this subsection for a fraudulent purpose; or

(D) the environmental audit report, finding, opinion, or other communication was prepared for the purpose of avoiding disclosure of information required for an investigative, administrative, or judicial proceeding that, at the time of preparation, was imminent or in progress.

(b) EXCLUSIONS- Subsection (a) shall not apply to—

(1) a document or other information required to be developed, maintained, or reported pursuant to a Federal environmental law;

(2) a document or other information required to be available to a Federal agency or a State agency designated to carry out a regulatory activity pursuant to a Federal environmental law;

(3) information obtained by a Federal agency or State agency referred to in paragraph (2) through observation, sampling, or monitoring; or

(4) information obtained by a Federal agency or State agency referred to in paragraph (2) through an independent source.

SECTION 5. TESTIMONY.

Notwithstanding any other provision of law, a person or entity, including any officer or employee of the person or entity, that performs a voluntary environmental self-evaluation may not be required to give testimony in a Federal court or an administrative proceeding of a Federal agency without the consent of the person or entity concerning the voluntary environmental self-evaluation, including an environmental audit report, finding, opinion, or other communication with respect to which section 3(a) applies.

SECTION 6. DISCLOSURES.

(a) IN GENERAL- The disclosure of information relating to a Federal environmental law to the appropriate official of a Federal or State agency responsible for administering a Federal environmental law shall be considered to be a voluntary disclosure if—

(1) the disclosure of information arises out of a voluntary environmental self-evaluation;

(2) the person or entity that initiates the self-evaluation—

(A) ensures that the disclosure is made promptly after receiving knowledge of the information referred to in paragraph (1); and

(B) initiates an action to address the issues identified in the disclosure—

(i) within a reasonable period of time after receiving knowledge of the information; and

(ii) within a period of time that is adequate to achieve compliance with the requirements of the Federal environmental law that is the subject of the action (including submitting an application for an applicable permit); and

(3) the person or entity that makes the disclosure provides any further relevant information requested, as a result of the disclosure, by the appropriate official of the Federal or State agency responsible for administering the Federal environmental law.

(b) INVOLUNTARY DISCLOSURES- For the purposes of this Act, a disclosure of information to an appropriate official of a Federal or State agency responsible for administering a Federal environmental law shall not be considered to be a voluntary disclosure if the person or government entity making the disclosure has been found by a Federal or State court to have committed a pattern of significant violations of Federal or State laws, or orders on consent, related to environmental quality, due to separate and distinct events giving rise to the violations, during the 3-year period prior to the date of disclosure.

(c) PRESUMPTION OF APPLICABILITY- If a person or entity makes a disclosure other than a disclosure referred to in subsection (b) of a violation of a Federal environmental law to an appropriate official of a Federal or State agency responsible for administering the Federal environmental law—

(1) there shall be a presumption that the disclosure is a voluntary disclosure, if the person or entity provides information supporting a claim that the information is a voluntary disclosure at the time the person or entity makes the disclosure; and

(2) until such time as the presumption is rebutted, the person or entity shall be immune from any administrative, civil, or criminal penalty for the violation.

(d) REBUTTAL OF PRESUMPTION-

(1) IN GENERAL- The head of a Federal or State agency described in subsection (c) shall have the burden of rebutting a presumption established under such subsection. If the head of the Federal or State agency fails to rebut the presumption pursuant to this subsection—

(A) the head of the Federal or State agency may not assess an administrative penalty against a person or entity described in subsection (c) with respect to the violation by the person or entity and may not issue a cease and desist order for the violation; and

(B) no Federal or State court may assess a civil penalty or criminal negligence penalty against the person or entity for the violation.

(2) REBUTTAL- In order to rebut a presumption referred to in subsection (c), the appropriate official of a Federal or State agency responsible for administering the Federal environmental law that is the subject of a violation referred to in such subsection shall be required to demonstrate, on the basis of the factors described in subsection (a), and to the satisfaction of the head of the Federal or State agency, that the disclosure is not a voluntary disclosure. If the disclosure is made directly to the head of the Federal or State agency, the head of the Federal or State agency shall apply the factors described in subsection (a) in rebutting the presumption. A decision made by the head of the Federal agency under this paragraph shall constitute a final agency action.

(e) STATUTORY CONSTRUCTION- Except as expressly provided in this section, nothing in this section is intended to affect the authority of a Federal or State agency responsible for administering a Federal environmental law to carry out any requirement of the law associated with information disclosed in a voluntary disclosure.

GLOSSARY

GLOSSARY

Abatement - Reducing the degree or intensity of, or eliminating, pollution.

Accident Site - The location of an unexpected occurrence, failure or loss, either at a plant or along a transportation route, resulting in a release of hazardous materials.

Acclimatization - The physiological and behavioral adjustments of an organism to changes in its environment.

Acid Rain - A complex chemical and atmospheric phenomenon that occurs when emissions of sulfur and nitrogen compounds and other substances are transformed by chemical processes in the atmosphere, often far from the original sources, and then deposited on earth in either wet or dry form. The wet forms, popularly called "acid rain," can fall as rain, snow, or fog. The dry forms are acidic gases or particulates.

Acidic - The condition of water or soil that contains a sufficient amount of acid substances to lower the pH below 7.0

Active Ingredient - In any pesticide product, the component that kills, or otherwise controls, target pests.

Acute Toxicity - The ability of a substance to cause poisonous effects resulting in severe biological harm or death soon after a single exposure or dose.

Adaptation - Changes in an organism's structure or habits that help it adjust to its surroundings.

Administrative Order - A legal document signed by EPA directing an individual, business, or other entity to take corrective action or refrain from an activity.

Administrative Procedures Act - A law that spells out procedures and requirements related to the promulgation of regulations.

Aeration - A process which promotes biological degradation of organic matter in water.

Aeration Tank - A chamber used to inject air into water.

Aerosol - A suspension of liquid or solid particles in a gas.

Affected Public - The people who live and/or work near a hazardous waste site.

Agricultural Pollution - Farming wastes, including runoff and leaching of pesticides and fertilizers; erosion and dust from plowing; improper disposal of animal manure and carcasses; crop residues, and debris.

Air Contaminant - Any particulate matter, gas, or combination thereof, other than water vapor.

Air Pollutant - Any substance in air that could, in high enough concentration, harm man, other animals, vegetation, or material.

Air Pollution Control Device - Mechanism or equipment that cleans emissions generated by an incinerator by removing pollutants that would otherwise be released to the atmosphere.

Air Pollution - The presence of contaminant or pollutant substances in the air that do not disperse properly and interfere with human health or welfare, or produce other harmful environmental effects.

Air Quality Criteria - The levels of pollution and lengths of exposure above which adverse health and welfare effects may occur.

Air Toxics - Any air pollutant for which a national ambient air quality standard (NAAQS) does not exist that may reasonably be anticipated to cause cancer, developmental effects, reproductive dysfunctions, neurological disorders, heritable gene mutations, or other serious or irreversible chronic or acute health effects in humans.

Airborne Particulates - Total suspended particulate matter found in the atmosphere as solid particles or liquid droplets.

Airborne Release - Release of any chemical into the air.

Algae - Simple rootless plants that grow in sunlit waters in proportion to the amount of available nutrients. They can affect water quality adversely by lowering the dissolved oxygen in the water.

Alkaline - The condition of water or soil which contains a sufficient amount of alkali substance to raise the pH above 7.0.

Alkalinity - The capacity of water to neutralize acids.

Alternative Fuels - Substitutes for traditional liquid, oil-derived motor vehicle fuels like gasoline and diesel. Includes methanol, ethanol, compressed natural gas, and others.

Ambient Air - Any unconfined portion of the atmosphere - open air, surrounding air.

Aquifer - An underground geological formation, or group of formations, containing usable amounts of groundwater that can supply wells and springs.

Asbestos - A mineral fiber that can pollute air or water and cause cancer or asbestosis when inhaled.

Asbestosis - A disease associated with inhalation of asbestos fibers. The disease makes breathing progressively more difficult and can be fatal.

Assay - A test for a particular chemical or effect.

Assimilation - The ability of a body of water to purify itself of pollutants.

Attainment Area - An area considered to have air quality as good as or better than the national ambient air quality standards as defined in the Clean Air Act.

Background Level - In air pollution control, the concentration of air pollutants in a definite area during a fixed period of time prior to the starting up or on the stoppage of a source of emission under control.

Bacteria - Microscopic living organisms that can aid in pollution control by metabolizing organic matter in sewage, oil spills or other pollutants. However, bacteria in soil, water or air can also cause human, animal and plant health problems.

BEN - EPA's computer model for analyzing a violator's economic gain from not complying with the law.

Biodegradable - Capable of decomposing rapidly under natural conditions.

Biological Control - In pest control, the use of animals and organisms that eat or otherwise kill or out-compete pests.

Biological Treatment - A treatment technology that uses bacteria to consume organic waste.

Biomass - All of the living material in a given area; often refers to vegetation.

Biosphere - The portion of Earth and its atmosphere that can support life.

Biotic Community - A naturally occurring assemblage of plants and animals that live in the same environment and are mutually sustaining and interdependent.

Blackwater - Water that contains animal, human, or food waste.

Blood Products - Any product derived from human blood, including but not limited to blood plasma, platelets, red or white corpuscles, and derived licensed products such as interferon.

Bog - A type of wetland that accumulates appreciable peat deposits. Bogs depend primarily on precipitation for their water source, and are usually acidic and rich in plant residue with a conspicuous mat of living green moss.

Bottom Land Hardwoods - Forested freshwater wetlands adjacent to rivers in the southeastern United States, especially valuable for wildlife breeding, nesting and habitat.

Burial Ground - A disposal site for radioactive waste materials that uses earth or water as a shield.

Cap - A layer of clay, or other impermeable material installed over the top of a closed landfill to prevent entry of rainwater and minimize leachate.

Capacity Assurance Plan - A statewide plan which supports a state's ability to manage the hazardous waste generated within its boundaries over a twenty year period.

Carbon Monoxide (CO) - A colorless, odorless, poisonous gas produced by incomplete fossil fuel combustion.

Carcinogen - Any substance that can cause or aggravate cancer.

Characteristic - Any one of the four categories used in defining hazardous waste - ignitability, corrosivity, reactivity, and toxicity.

Chemical Treatment - Any one of a variety of technologies that use chemicals or a variety of chemical processes to treat waste.

Chlorinated Hydrocarbons - These include a class of persistent, broad-spectrum insecticides that linger in the environment and accumulate in the food chain.

Chlorination - The application of chlorine to drinking water, sewage, or industrial waste to disinfect or to oxidize undesirable compounds.

Chlorofluorocarbons (CFCs) - A family of inert, nontoxic, and easily liquified chemicals used in refrigeration, air conditioning, packaging, insulation, or as solvents and aerosol propellants.

Chronic Toxicity - The capacity of a substance to cause long-term poisonous human health effects.

Clarifier - A tank in which solids settle to the bottom and are subsequently removed as sludge.

Clean Fuels - Blends or substitutes for gasoline fuels, including compressed natural gas, methanol, ethanol, liquified petroleum gas, and others.

Cleanup - Actions taken to deal with a release or threat of release of a hazardous substance that could affect humans and/or the environment.

Coliform Index - A rating of the purity of water based on a count of fecal bacteria.

Coliform Organism - Microorganisms found in the intestinal tract of humans and animals.

Commercial Waste - All solid wastes emanating from business establishments such as stores, markets, office buildings, restaurants, shopping centers, and theaters.

Decontamination - Removal of harmful substances such as noxious chemicals, harmful bacteria or other organisms, or radioactive material from exposed individuals, rooms and furnishings in buildings, or the exterior environment.

Deep-Well Injection - Deposition of raw or treated, filtered hazardous waste by pumping it into deep wells, where it is contained in the pores of permeable subsurface rock.

Defluoridation - The removal of excess fluoride in drinking water to prevent the staining of teeth.

Defoliant - An herbicide that removes leaves from trees and growing plants.

DES - A synthetic estrogen, diethylstilbestrol is used as a growth stimulant in food animals. Residues in meat are thought to be carcinogenic.

Designated Pollutant - An air pollutant which is neither a criteria nor hazardous pollutant, as described in the Clean Air Act, but for which new source performance standards exist.

Direct Runoff - Water that flows over the ground surface or through the ground directly into streams, rivers, and lakes.

Ecological Impact - The effect that a man-made or natural activity has on living organisms and their non-living environment.

Ecology - The relationship of living things to one another and their environment, or the study of such relationships.

Emission - Pollution discharged into the atmosphere from smokestacks, other vents, and surface areas of commercial or industrial facilities; from residential chimneys; and from motor vehicle, locomotive, or aircraft exhausts.

Emission Standard - The maximum amount of air polluting discharge legally allowed from a single source, mobile or stationary.

Endangered Species - Animals, birds, fish, plants, or other living organisms threatened with extinction by man-made or natural changes in their environment.

Environmental Impact Statement - A document required of federal agencies by the National Environmental Policy Act for major projects or legislative proposals significantly affecting the environment.

Environmental Justice - The fair treatment of all races, cultures, incomes, and educational levels with respect to the development, implementation, and enforcement of environmental laws, regulations, and policies.

Feasibility Study - Analysis of the practicability of a proposal.

Fecal Coliform Bacteria - Bacteria found in the intestinal tracts of mammals. Their presence in water or sludge is an indicator of pollution and possible contamination by pathogens.

Fen - A type of wetland that accumulates peat deposits. Fens are less acidic than bogs, deriving most of their water from groundwater rich in calcium and magnesium.

FIFRA Pesticide Ingredient - An ingredient of a pesticide that must be registered with EPA under the Federal Insecticide, fungicide, and Rodenticide Act.

Floodplain - The flat or nearly flat land along a river or stream or in a tidal area that is covered by water during a flood.

Fluoridation - The addition of a chemical to increase the concentration of fluoride ions drinking water to reduce the incidence of tooth decay in children.

Fluorocarbons (FCs) - Any of a number of organic compounds analogous to hydrocarbons in which one or more hydrogen atoms are replaced by fluorine.

Fossil Fuel - Fuel derived from ancient organic remains, e.g., peat, coal, crude oil, and natural gas.

Fresh Water - Water that generally contains less than 1,000 milligrams-per liter of dissolved solids,

Fungicide - Pesticides which are used to control, deter, or destroy fungi.

Grab Sample - A single sample collected at a particular time and place that represents the composition of the water only at that time and place.

Greenhouse Effect - The warming of the Earth's atmosphere attributed to a build-up of carbon dioxide or other gases.

Ground Water - The supply of fresh water found beneath the Earth's surface, usually in aquifers, which supply wells and springs.

Habitat - The place where a population (e.g., human, animal, plant, microorganism) lives and its surroundings, both living and non-living.

Hazardous Air Pollutants - Air pollutants which are not covered by ambient air quality standards but which, as defined in the Clean Air Act, may reasonably be expected to cause or contribute to irreversible illness or death.

Hazardous Substance - Any material that poses a threat to human health and/or the environment.

Hazardous Waste - By-products of society that can pose a substantial or potential hazard to human health or the environment when improperly managed.

Health Advisory Level - A non-regulatory health-based reference level of chemical traces in drinking water at which there are no adverse health risks when ingested over various periods of time.

Hydrocarbons (HC) - Chemical compounds that consist entirely of carbon and hydrogen.

Indoor Air Pollution - Chemical, physical, or biological contaminants in indoor air.

Infectious Waste - Hazardous waste with infectious characteristics, including - contaminated animal waste; human blood and blood products; isolation waste, pathological waste; and discarded sharps instruments.

Landfills - Sanitary disposal sites for non-hazardous solid wastes spread in layers, compacted to the smallest practical volume, and covered by material applied at the end of each operating day. Secure chemical landfills are disposal sites for hazardous waste, selected and designed to minimize the chance of release of hazardous substances into the environment.

Mandatory Recycling - Programs which by law require consumers to separate trash so that some or all recyclable materials are recovered for recycling rather than going to landfills.

Maximum Contaminant Level - The maximum permissible level of a contaminant in water delivered to any user of a public system.

Mitigation - Measures taken to reduce adverse impacts on the environment.

Mobile Source - Any non-stationary source of air pollution such as cars, trucks, motorcycles, buses, airplanes, locomotives.

Morbidity - Rate of disease incidence.

National Ambient Air Quality Standards (NAAQS) -Standards established by EPA that apply for outside air throughout the country.

National Pollutant Discharge Elimination System (NPDES) - A provision of the Clean Water Act which prohibits discharge of pollutants into waters of the United States unless a special permit is issued by EPA, a state, or, where delegated, a tribal government on an Indian reservation.

National Response Team (NRT) - Representatives of 13 federal agencies that, as a team, coordinate federal responses to nationally significant incidents of pollution—an oil spill, a major chemical release, or a Superfund response action—and provide advice and technical assistance to the responding agency(ies) before and during a response action.

Navigable Waters - Traditionally, waters sufficiently deep and wide for navigation by all, or specified vessels; such waters in the United States come under federal jurisdiction and are protected by certain provisions of the Clean Water Act.

NOx - Product of combustion from transportation and stationary sources and a major contributor to the formation of ozone in the troposphere and to acid deposition.

Non-Attainment Area - Area that does not meet one or more of the National Ambient Air Quality Standards for the criteria pollutants designated in the Clean Air Act.

Oil Spill - An accidental or intentional discharge of oil which reaches bodies of water.

Ozone Hole - Thinning break in the stratospheric ozone layer.

Ozone Layer - The protective layer in the atmosphere, about 15 miles above the ground, that absorbs some of the sun's ultraviolet rays, thereby reducing the amount of potentially harmful radiation reaching the earth's surface.

Particulates - Fine liquid or solid particles such as dust, smoke, mist, fumes, or smog found in air or emissions.

Permit - An authorization, license, or equivalent control document issued by EPA or an approved state agency to implement the requirements of an environmental regulation.

Pesticide - Substances or mixture there of intended for preventing, destroying, repelling, or mitigating any pest.

pH - An expression of the intensity of the basic or acid condition of a liquid.

Pollutant - Generally, any substance introduced into the environment that adversely affects the usefulness of a resource.

Pollutant Standard Index (PSI) - Measure of adverse health effects of air pollution levels in major cities.

Pollution - Generally, the presence of matter or energy whose nature, location, or quantity produces undesired environmental effects.

Polyvinyl Chloride (PVC) - A tough, environmentally indestructible plastic that releases hydrochloric acid when burned.

Primary Drinking Water Regulation - Applies to public water systems and specifies a contaminant level, which, in the judgment of the EPA Administrator, will not adversely affect human health.

Raw Sewage - Untreated wastewater and its contents.

Recommended Maximum Contaminant Level (RMCL) - The maximum level of a contaminant in drinking water at which no known or anticipated adverse affect on human health would occur.

Recycle - Minimizing waste generation by recovering and reprocessing usable products that might otherwise become waste.

Regional Response Team (RRT) - Representatives of federal, local, and state agencies who may assist in coordination of activities at the request of the On-Scene Coordinator before and during a significant pollution incident such as an oil spill, major chemical release, or a Superfund response.

Release - Any spilling, leaking, pumping, pouring, emitting, emptying, discharging, injecting, escaping, leaching, dumping, or disposing into the environment of a hazardous or toxic chemical or extremely hazardous substance.

Reportable Quantity (RQ) - Quantity of a hazardous substance that triggers reports under CERCLA.

Risk - A measure of the probability that damage to life, health, property, and/or the environment will occur as a result of a given hazard.

Salt Water Intrusion - The invasion of fresh surface or ground water by salt water.

Salvage - The utilization of waste materials.

Secondary Drinking Water Regulations - Non-enforceable regulations applying to public water systems and specifying the maximum contamination levels that, in the judgment of EPA, are required to protect the public welfare.

Septic Tank - An underground storage tank for wastes from homes not connected to a sewer line. Waste goes directly from the home to the tank.

Sewage - The waste and wastewater produced by residential and commercial sources and discharged into sewers.

Sewer - A channel or conduit that carries wastewater and storm-water runoff from the source to a treatment plant or receiving stream.

Smog - Air pollution associated with oxidants.

Solid Waste Management - Supervised handling of waste materials from their source through recovery processes to disposal.

State Emergency Response Commission (SERC) -Commission appointed by each state governor according to the requirements of SARA Title III.

State Implementation Plans (SIP) - EPA approved state plans for the establishment, regulation, and enforcement of air pollution standards.

Stationary Source - A fixed-site producer of pollution, mainly power plants and other facilities using industrial combustion processes.

Storm Sewer - A system of pipes that carries only water runoff from buildings and land surfaces.

Strip-Mining - A process that uses machines to scrape soil or rock away from mineral deposits just under the earth's surface.

Superfund - The program operated under the legislative authority of CERCLA and SARA that funds and carries out EPA solid waste emergency and long-term removal and remedial activities.

Surface Runoff - Precipitation, snow melt, or irrigation in excess of what can infiltrate the soil surface and be stored in small surface depressions; a major transporter of nonpoint source pollutants.

Toxic Substance - A chemical or mixture that may present an unreasonable risk of injury to health or the environment.

Toxic Waste - A waste that can produce injury if inhaled, swallowed, or absorbed through the skin.

Treated Wastewater - Wastewater that has been subjected to one or more physical, chemical, and biological processes to reduce its pollution of health hazards.

Treatment Plant - A structure built to treat wastewater before discharging it into the environment.

Trust Fund (CERCLA) - A fund set up under the Comprehensive Environmental Response, Compensation and Liability Act (CERCLA) to help pay for cleanup of hazardous waste sites and for legal action to force those responsible for the sites to clean them up.

Ultraviolet Rays - Radiation from the sun that can be useful or potentially harmful. UV rays from one part of the spectrum (UV-A) enhance plant life and are useful in some medical and dental procedures; UV rays from other parts of the spectrum (UV-B) can cause skin cancer or other tissue damage.

Underground Injection Control (UIC) - The program under the Safe Drinking Water Act that regulates the use of wells to pump fluids into the ground.

Underground Storage Tank - A tank located at least partially underground and designed to hold gasoline or other petroleum products or chemicals.

Urban Runoff - Storm water from city streets and adjacent domestic or commercial properties that carries pollutants of various kinds into the sewer systems and receiving waters.

Volatile Organic Compound (VOC) - Any organic compound that participates in atmospheric photochemical reactions except those designated by EPA as having negligible photochemical reactivity.

Waste - Unwanted materials left over from a manufacturing process or refuse from places of human or animal habitation.

Wastewater - The spent or used water from a home, community, farm, or industry that contains dissolved or suspended matter.

Water Pollution - The presence in water of enough harmful or objectionable material to damage the water's quality.

Watershed - The land area that drains into a stream; the watershed for a major river may encompass a number of smaller watersheds that ultimately combine at a common delivery point.

Zooplankton - Tiny aquatic animals eaten by fish.

SOURCE - U.S. ENVIRONMENTAL PROTECTION AGENCY

BIBLIOGRAPHY AND ADDITIONAL READING

BIBLIOGRAPHY AND ADDITIONAL READING

Bregman, Jacob I. and Mackenthun, Kenneth M. *Environmental Regulations Handbook*. Boca Raton, FL: Lewis Publishing Company, 1992.

Miller, Jeffrey G. *Citizen Suits: Private Enforcement of Federal Pollution Control Laws*. New York, NY: Wiley Law Publications, 1987.

Reitze, Arnold W. *Air Pollution Law*. Charlottesville, VA: Michie Butterworth Publishing Company, 1995.

Vaughan, Ray *Essentials of Environmental Law*. Rockville, MD: Government Institutes, 1994.

The United States Environmental Protection Agency (Date Visited: October 1997) http://www/epa.gov/.